New Believers Discipleship

Teachings and Practices for the Christian Journey

Ajilon Ferdinand

Reason Publishing

ISBN: 978-1-990266-21-8

Published by
Reason with Robdon
Essex SS68SU, UK
+447308523252
reasonwithrobdon@gmail.com

Author's Contact Information
1 (876) 434-6300
ajaferdi@gmail.com
ajaferdi@yahoo.com

Table of Contents

Acknowledgements

I use this opportunity to thank Lora Chinpenn from the New Testament Church of God, Mile End, for her help during the initial testing and implementation of this guidebook. Thanks to Dr. Roy Notice for his insightful feedback on the themes and other content details for this resource. Thanks to Ronamae Bradford for her editorial work and perceptive recommendations. I am especially thankful for my wife, Kareen, who provided invaluable support in this process.

—Ajilon Ferdinand—

INTRODUCTION

But grow in the grace and knowledge of our Lord and Savior Jesus Christ. To him be the glory both now and to the day of eternity. Amen." (2 Peter 3:18 NRSV)

The Bible urges all believers to grow in the grace and knowledge of our Lord Jesus. The effect of such growth is that believers will increase in practical godliness, resulting in a life of real discipleship. Practical godliness involves cultivating personal spiritual disciplines (such as Bible reading, prayer, fasting, etc.) and corporate disciplines (fellowship, worship, baptism, Lord's Supper etc.). Although the Spirit works in us to produce the character of Christ, growth in godliness is not automatic.

To attain spiritual growth, each believer has to take the journey of training in godliness. The key to godliness is your intentional preparation and on-going participation in the Christian community. Sadly, in many local churches, the preparation of new believers for the Christian journey has largely been omitted or the process lacks structure and focus. The consequence of an unplanned discipleship approach is that many new believers eventually fall away from the faith within their first few months, or year of becoming a Christian. This is not something I want to happen to you. I want you to stay and grow in your faith. Your calling and life as a disciple is too precious for you to take this journey of a lifetime without the resources to thrive as you go and grow. That is where this guidebook comes in.

This guidebook is your training resource for the journey ahead. I initially created it while I was pastoring the New Testament Church of God in Mile End, St. Ann. Over a period of six years, the discipleship program there had a retention rate of 99% of all new disciples that were baptized. When I was appointed as the associate pastor at a much larger church in the city of Kingston, the New Testament Church of God at 65 Waltham Park Road, I also utilized this resource there. In the first year we had a 90% retention rate (and were able to account for the other 10%). It is currently in progress at the Papine New Testament Church of God, where I now serve as pastor, and I see similar results at that church.

I want to share this resource with you because it works. In this guidebook you will take a journey that spans three stages, covering various discipleship essentials, practices, and core teachings of our faith. You will encounter personal life applications, discussion questions, and simple weekly exercises that will shape your heart as a disciple. The special features in this book include a weekly Bible reading schedule, devotional model, a fasting schedule, and a spiritual maturity assessment to track your growth at the end of this process. As you begin your Christian journey, take this book with you. I offer it to you now, at this stage of your walk of faith, with the heartiest sentiments that one day you will help me see Christ more fully than I now do.

—Ajilon Ferdinand

HOW TO USE THIS GUIDEBOOK

This guidebook is designed to be used by the teacher and student disciple. It follows a three-stage spiritual development process on a session-to-session basis—one lesson at a time, usually weekly. The lessons are written in such a way that they do not require extensive explanations. The teacher should exercise restraint in offering widespread clarifications on every line that appears important. This does not mean the teacher cannot divert to answer questions or make important applications that will help the new disciples.

It is also important to note that most of the lessons end with practical applications, a discussion, and weekly assignments. The teacher must encourage students to complete the assignments. A review of the assignment should be done before moving forward with a new lesson. The teacher should also assess the readiness of the student to move on to each new stage. A special feature of this guidebook and program is that every stage ends with an event. The idea is to create a sense of progress and anticipation throughout this initial discipleship process.

The stages

Stage One – covers themes to help the new convert make the journey from conversion to baptism. At the end of stage one, the new convert will gain a sense of understanding of the basic teachings about salvation and be prepared for baptism. The focus here is to end this stage with baptism.

Stage Two – considers various biblical themes and practical disciplines to help the new believer grow in the Christian faith. At the end of this stage, each convert will take part in a one-week guided fast. The fast is intended to give convert practical experiences in this important Christian discipline.

Stage Three – explores some core beliefs of Pentecostalism, the church, and the New Testament Church of God. At the end of this stage, converts will complete a short spiritual growth assessment and express a willingness for membership in the local church.

Commitments

Each new convert should be faithful in attending the classes, be on time, and actively participate in the classes. All participants should be sensitive and respectful to the insights and thoughts of others. All questions and comments are valuable, so each disciple should show courtesy and thoughtfulness toward each other. The ideal number of converts per class is between ten to fifteen. If the number is higher than fifteen the discipleship mentor should divide the converts into two groups.

Desired outcome

The goal of the discipleship process is to make disciples of all believers. Once a new believer completes this program, the new believer should be prepared for formal membership within the local church and for a life of practical godliness.

STAGE ONE

Discipleship Essentials

LESSON 1

Becoming a Christian

Scripture: Matthew 18:3; Acts 3:19
Central Point: *We become Christians when we repent of our sins and trust in Jesus as our Savior.*

Introduction

As we begin this journey, we will be exploring the idea of becoming a Christian. We need to know what we mean when we say, "I am a Christian" and understand how we become Christians. The Bible teaches us that the Christian life is made possible by the gift of salvation through Jesus Christ. Salvation is a life changing experience. It is a gift from God to all believers. Once you have decided to accept Jesus, the next step is to follow through with a life of obedience to him.

Who is a Christian?

A Christian is a devoted follower or disciple of Jesus Christ. The word *Christian* itself means "a follower of Christ." Acts 3:36 tells us that "the disciples were called Christians first in Antioch," one of the cities in the Mediterranean region. A Christian is someone who lives a life of love and obedience to Jesus. Christians are also referred to as disciples, the people of God, and many other titles. Being a member of a church, attending church, or giving to church does not make a person a Christian.

How does a person become a Christian?

To become a Christian, a person needs to believe in Jesus as Savior, fully accepting His death as the sufficient sacrifice for sin and trusting in Him for salvation.

This is usually accomplished in two steps:

First, repent of all sin. The Apostle Peter commanded a crowd, "Repent ye therefore, and be converted, that your sins may be blotted out" (Acts 3:19). Repentance means to change one's mind from rebellion to one of obedience toward God, while conversion is to turn one's life over to God. Repentance is to change the attitude of your mind by admitting we have sinned against God. Conversion means to change the moral direction of your life to follow God's will and live for Him.

Second, accept Jesus as Lord. Romans 10:9-10 says, "If you confess with thy mouth the Lord Jesus, and shalt believe in thine heart that God hath raised him from the dead, thou shalt be saved." To receive salvation, one must profess or acknowledge that Jesus is Lord or master of your life. We accept Christ in our heart by saying yes to who He is as God's Son and what He has done to save us.

God has appointed the acts of repentance and acceptance of Jesus as the means of becoming a Christian. No one can repent or accept Jesus on our behalf. Becoming a Christian depends on your personal choice. It is that simple! Your personal belief in Jesus leads to the gift of salvation.

The gift of Salvation

What is Salvation? The word salvation refers to our deliverance. Deliverance from what? Deliverance from God's wrath as the penalty for sin. Believers are "saved from the wrath of God" (Romans 5:9). Salvation also means deliverance from anything that oppresses human life.

When the Bible speaks about salvation as a gift, it emphasizes that it is something willingly given to us rather than something we earn. Salvation is not earned by human efforts; it is a gift from God. A common but accurate definition describes grace as the "unmerited favor of God toward man." Grace flows from God's heart of compassion.

The Lord is gracious; it is not His desire for anyone to perish or face His wrath. The Bible says, "For God hath not appointed us to wrath, but to obtain salvation by our Lord Jesus Christ" (I Thessalonians 5:9). Only

God can deliver us from the penalty of sin. The penalty of sin is death, both spiritual and physical death.

The message of Salvation

Salvation is a gift from God to us. God's plan of salvation was developed from the beginning of human history and found its center in the person of Jesus. The message of salvation has four basic components:

1. God created everything for His pleasure. God freely and lovingly "created the heavens and the earth" (Genesis 1:1) and "made us in His image" (1:26-27). God is completely responsible for all creation, including human life. He created everything for His pleasure and to work in harmony with His will.

2. Humanity sinned against God. Sin is an act of human disobedience against God. Romans 3:23 says, "all have sinned and come short of the glory of God." The Bible says before coming to Christ, "We were dead in trespasses and sins" (Ephesians 2:1). Sin gives rise to spiritual death, a form of separation from God, and a disruption in our relationship with Him. In a state of spiritual death, we are unable to save ourselves from sin.

3. Jesus is our only Savior. Jesus Christ is God's solution to the human problem of sin. "God commendeth His love toward us, in that, while we were yet sinners, Christ died for us" (Romans 5:8). Jesus became a man, died on the cross, and rose from the dead to save us from sin and death. Jesus Christ, the Son of God, is the only one qualified to be our Savior.

4. We are saved by grace through faith. "For by grace are ye saved through faith; and that not of yourselves: it is the gift of God" (Ephesians 2:8). Grace is God's favor towards us. Salvation comes through our faith in Jesus, by God's grace. Faith is the act of believing. Faith itself does not cause salvation but is the "way or means" appointed by God for a person to receive salvation.

These four components represent the message of salvation. The message is simple:

a. God created us.
b. We sinned against God.
c. Jesus died to save us.
d. We are saved from sin by God's grace through our faith.

The message of the gospel is the good news of hope through Jesus Christ. It is "the power of God unto salvation to everyone that believeth" (Romans 1:16).

What happens when you become a Christian?

Becoming a Christian is a process of change. What happens in us is nothing short of a spiritual miracle. There are three Bible expressions that we can use to help us understand the work of God within us.

1. First, God redeems us. The word redemption means "to buy back." When we talk about Christ redeeming us, we are suggesting He paid the price to bring us back to God. That was the first work Jesus did. 1 Peter 1:18-19 says, "Forasmuch as ye know that ye were not redeemed with corruptible things, as silver and gold, from your vain conversation received by tradition from your fathers; But with the precious blood of Christ, as of a lamb without blemish and without spot."

2. Next, God regenerates us. This means you are born again, spiritually. It is not something that originates with human action. The Holy Spirit works in us to change the attitude of our soul and makes us new creations. John 3:5 states, "Except a man be born of water, and of the Spirit, he cannot enter into the kingdom of God." This blessing is a unique act of God.

3. Then, God justifies us. This means you are not guilty anymore. Your sins are forgiven; you are acquitted. Justification is the word we use to explain the pardoning and removal of sins from an offender's life. Romans 3:24 clarifies this, "Therefore being justified by faith, we have peace with God through our Lord Jesus Christ."

The emphasis here is not on the sequence or order of those events. The idea here is to show you the effects of God's work in your life. When we become Christians, God changes our lives for the better. He takes us His children, awakens us from death to new life in Christ, and forgives our all our sins.

Summary and Life Application

A Christian is a follower of Jesus. You become a Christian by repenting of your sins and accepting Jesus as Lord. Salvation is deliverance from sin; it is a free gift of God's grace. It is God's gift, made available to us through the death of Jesus Christ. When we believe the message of salvation, God saves us and turns our life around. How should we respond to God's grace? Let us be thankful for this gift of grace because God through Christ has forgiven all our sins. If that is true about you, your life as a Christian has already begun. Keep in mind that your walk with God started the moment you repented and accepted Jesus as your Savior and Lord. You must now seek to forsake your past sinful lifestyle entirely. If God through the Spirit saved you, know that you are saved. No one can change or deny that truth. How do you move forward from this point? Your job is to now believe that you have salvation within and live like a believer.

Sincerely respond to these clarification questions:

1. Have you confessed your sins, trusted in God for forgiveness, and accepted Jesus as your personal Savior?

2. If you believe that God has forgiven you, are you now willing to draw closer to Him through our discipleship classes? Raise your hands if you are saying, "Yes, today I am deciding to follow Jesus!"

3. Does the following statement apply to you? "I prayed the "sinner's prayer", but I am not 100% ready to be a Christian. I am not ready to commit to becoming a full-time disciple."

4. Does the following statement apply to you? I want to change my life, but I have some personal situations that will prevent me from fully committing to Christ. I need time and help to work through some personal matters.

LESSON 1—WEEKLY ASSIGNMENT

Use this week to spend some time in prayer, talking with God about your decision. Allow your mind to be fully convinced about following Jesus. If you need more time, request to have a meeting with the disciple leader or pastor, so they can offer you further guidance. Plan to be present at the next session to continue your journey of transformation.

LESSON 2

A New Life in Christ

Scripture: 2 Corinthians 5:17-18
Central Point: *Those who receive Christ also receive a new life and a renewed fellowship with God.*

Introduction

The theme of newness or renewal is a strand of teaching that began in the Old Testament. It forms part of God's intentions to "create new heavens and a new earth" (Isaiah 65:17). This was due to the simple fact that sin disrupted God's original creation. God's original creation was corrupted when Adam and Eve sinned and were judged by God. Christ paid the price to restore our broken relationship with God. Believing in Jesus makes us part of this new creation of God. Our focus for today will be on what it means to be a new creation in Christ. Let us begin by considering what it means to be a new creation in Christ.

New creation in Christ

If anyone is in Christ, he is a *new creation*. Our encounter with Jesus the Savior makes our life brand new. That does not mean old habits, evil thoughts, and lustful feelings are altogether gone, and everything becomes literally new. Practically, that is not the case—it is not true.

When a person comes to be "in Christ" by faith, this experience signals the beginning of a restored life. God totally restructures the life of a believer, altering the whole fabric of their being—thinking, feeling, and acting. This new work of God is so powerful that the Apostle Paul says it is like passing from one old existence into a new.

In 2 Corinthians 5:17 he explains, "Therefore if any man be in Christ, he is a new creature: old things are passed away; behold, all things are become new. Old things and habits pass away as we progress in our relationship with God in Jesus.

Christian author Charles Stanley comments on this verse. He says, "The new birth experience is exactly what God says it is—a fresh beginning. When we are born again, we not only have our sin forgiven and our guilt removed, but we also receive the Holy Spirit—who comes to indwell us and live Christ's life through us. We can never be what we were before because we have been born into His life—with new spirit and nature. And because of that, our desires and goals should be conformed to those that God has for us" (NASB, *Life Principles Notes*).

The new realities of your Life

Your new life in Christ is a form of spiritual transformation. Whenever a person becomes part of the body of Christ, God performs a new act of creation. There are three ways the "newness of life" comes into effect:

1. You now have a new spiritual life. This does not mean Christians are "super-beings" or that we can never sin again. It simply means the spiritual nature God intended for you to have before sin became a reality is restored in God's eyes. Our position in Christ makes it possible for us as believers to identify with him.

2. The light of the Gospel now shines in you. As a believer, the light of the gospel, which is the knowledge of God's glory, now shines in your heart. God has dispelled the darkness of sin, a form of chaos in human life. Just as God said, "Let there be light" at the beginning of creation, He has done that in you, making something new of your life.

3. You are now like Christ. Your *old man*—the old way of life—is destroyed by the creation of a new life unto God. The way of life that originates in Christ is transferred to you. Through the death of Christ, God has put a new spiritual nature unto you.

Our identification with Christ makes it possible to have a new life. Those three examples of a new life are real and present experiences. This means

God's original plan for your life is back on track. You are a new creation and now have a new way of looking at life. That is good news!

The blessings of your new Life in Christ

Your new life in Christ is a special experience. As a believer, you are the recipient of many spiritual blessings, which begin with your renewed relationship with God.

1. Being a "new creation" means that we have a renewed relationship with God. We are no longer strangers and foreigners to God. That truth applies to Christians all over the world. We "have peace with God through our Lord Jesus Christ" (Romans 5:1). Peace is an "inner rest of spirit." Peace points to our fellowship with God. It comes because we are no longer at war with God through a life of disobedience. You don't have to wait for the future to experience peace with God. The peace that God gives to you is not only real but something we experience in the present.

2. In addition, you have a new assurance in God. You are no longer alone in life. Jesus promised his disciples, "If a man loves me, he will keep my words: and my Father will love him, and we will come unto him, and make our abode with him" (John 14:23). If we love Jesus and obey God's word, He offers us a special assurance. You have the assurance of God's abiding presence in your life. This means you are never alone. God is always with you. He promises to be close to you. You are one of God's children, and the Holy Spirit of God dwells in you. How do you feel knowing that you are a child of God?

3. Furthermore, you have joined a new family. The Christian life is not a solitary life. The Bible affirms that when Jesus lives in you, it means you are a member of God's family. Romans 8 teaches that we have "received the Spirit of adoption" (v. 15) and "that we are children of God" (v. 17). As a Christian, you have joined a family of believers. The Apostle Paul writes this, "Now, therefore, ye are no more strangers and foreigners, but fellow citizens with the saints, and of the household of God" (Ephesians 2:19).

In John 15:11-16, Jesus says all believers are one and he commands us to love one another. This admonition means fellow Christians are your brothers and sisters in Christ. Many new believers are afraid of losing their friends and loved ones because of their decision to follow Christ. Though this might happen in some cases, God doesn't want you to lose your relatives and friends. He desires for them to witness your new life. Your family is now bigger than ever.

You can think of your life as being fully connected. You are joined to God through peace and a personal relationship. You are attached to God's abiding presence and all God's presence has to offer you daily. You are also connected to Christians everywhere. These are blessings from the Lord, and it is your new life in Christ that makes everything possible.

Summary and Life Application

God wants to deepen his relationship with you. He wants you to remain connected to Him. As you live your new life in Christ, make your fellowship with God a daily and personal commitment.

1. How do you feel about having a personal and peaceful relationship with God?
2. What do you now understand about what it means for you to be living a new life?
3. How should you relate to other Christians in comparison to your biological family?

As a new believer, you should thank God that you are no longer the same but a completely new person. You might not see the newness immediately but be assured God is working in you to bring about an extraordinary spiritual change. Your new life is not your own doing; it is hidden in Jesus Christ. That means Christ is the source of your new life, and who you are now can only be found in Jesus.

So, what must you do at this point? Make a firm commitment to never return to the old habits and practices of your former life. Resist the temptations to continue in your old habits. Allow yourself to feel the assurance that comes with your new friendship with God. Remember, you are never alone in this world. God is always with you, even when you don't readily sense His presence. Finally, learn to love your new spiritual family members as you love your biological family and friends. You ought to love and serve other believers, as they love and serve you. God has saved you to have fellowship with Him and with other members of the family of God. Your church family is a wonderful gift from God.

LESSON 2—WEEKLY ASSIGNMENT

Read Luke 14:25-33 where Jesus talks about what it means to be his disciple. Answer the following questions:

1. What is the cost of being a disciple (vs. 26, 27)?

 ____

 ____

2. In verses 28-29, why should a disciple sit down and count the cost of following Jesus?

 ____

 ____

3. In verses 28-31 what does Jesus compare the life of a disciple to and why do you think that is important?

 ____

 ____

 ____

PRAYER FOR THE WEEK

Lord, please help me to be confident that I have a secure and personal relationship with you. Let the Holy Spirit continue to help me make personal changes in my behavior and personal attitudes. My desire is to live a life that is pleasing to you. Father, please help me to love your people as they love me. Amen

LESSON 3

The Call to be a Disciple

Scripture: Matthew 4:18-19
Central Point: *The main aim of discipleship is to develop and grow into a life of Christlikeness.*

Introduction

Perhaps you've heard the story of the farmer's chicken who proposed to the cow to make the farmer breakfast. The farmer is a good and kind man. The cow joyfully agreed, "I'm in; let us do it. What will we give him?" The chicken replied, "I will supply the eggs, and you will supply the meat." Realizing the cost of the invitation, the cow replied, "For you, that's devotion, but for me, it means total sacrifice." Then the cow walked away. This fable leads us to ask, what does it mean to follow Christ? Most people are open to an invitation to commit to Christ, but they become intimidated when they think about the sacrifice it takes. Jesus calls on you to make a personal decision to follow Him but not to sacrifice yourself to death. Instead, the call to discipleship is the process by which a believer grows into Christlikeness. Discipleship is a learning process, not a death sentence.

Come, follow Me

In Matthew 4:19 and 9:9, Jesus said to His first disciples, "Follow me." That invitation was not merely a matter of physically walking in the steps of Jesus. Instead, Jesus called His disciples to observe his teachings, manner of thinking and living, so that they could eventually carry out His mission. As it was then, it is today a call to a life of personal commitment and devotion to Jesus.

Jesus' invitation to "Follow me" is aimed directly at you—on a personal level. The invitation is for you to become a disciple of Jesus. The call is urgent. It is, for now, this moment, not tomorrow. Some people make excuses to get away from the call: "This is not a convenient time for me," "My father is sick," "I am about to get married," "I just started school," or "I'm not quite ready."

Any would-be follower of Jesus would have to be willing to hand over their future to Christ and follow Him. That idea may seem like uncharted waters, but God knows the way. When Jesus says, "Follow me," He means come and seek to be Christ-like in word, deed, and affections.

What does it mean to be a Disciple?

The word disciple literally means "a learner." In Christianity, a disciple is someone who learns to follow the example and teachings of Jesus Christ. Initially, a disciple was a person who knew Jesus in the flesh and followed after Him—but after Jesus" ascension, those who were committed to following Jesus were also called disciples. If you are committed to Jesus, that is what you are and should seek to remain.

There are different images we can use to picture what it means to be a disciple of Jesus. A disciple is someone who has fully surrendered to Christ. This means you have made up your mind to live your entire life following the precepts of the Lord Jesus. In essence, a disciple is someone who obeys by putting God's word into action.

A disciple is also someone who does good works. We were not saved by works, but for works. "For we are his workmanship, created in Christ Jesus unto good works, which God hath before ordained that we should walk in them" (Ephesians 2:10). The work of discipleship is to make disciples.

The call to follow Jesus is a call to obedience (John 15:10). Obedience means compliance to God's word or commands. It is not to be done occasionally but should be a daily occupation of our lives. Jesus also invites us to love Him. In Luke 10:27 Jesus says, "You shall love the Lord your God with all your heart, and with all your soul, and with all your strength, and with all your mind…" Your love for God must be sincere and strong.

You should love God with your all and above every other creature, object, person, or idea. Luke 10:27 continues to say," *and* love your neighbour as yourself." As a disciple, you must learn to love others with a genuine heart. Learning to love others authentically is a significant part of what discipleship is all about.

Go make Disciples

Christians recognize Matthew 28:19-20 as the Great Commission. The Great Commission is the most important command of Jesus to the church. In Matthew 28:19-20, the risen Lord commanded His disciples: Go ye therefore, and teach all nations, baptizing them in the name of the Father, and of the Son, and of the Holy Ghost: Teaching them to observe all things whatsoever I have commanded you: and, lo, I am with you always, even unto the end of the world.

In verse 19, Jesus issues a powerful command to his followers, "Go!" What does that mean to you? He commands his disciples to go to all nations. The reason the church seeks to make disciples is a matter of obedience to Jesus. Jesus wants disciples from every nation. He wants everyone to follow his example by living a life of obedience to God.

Being and making disciples is a significant part of God's purposes for human life. Interestingly, Jesus" first words to His disciples were, "Come, follow me," and His last words to them were, "Go, and make disciples." The life of a disciple is not aimless but purposeful.

We follow Jesus to learn His ways and manner of living, and as we do so, we serve His purposes in the world. As you grow in confidence through your faith, the commission of Jesus authorises you to reach others and call them to Christ, that they too might follow Him. The Great Commission directs us (as individuals and the church in general) to go and make disciples.

What is the goal of Discipleship?

Discipleship is God's way of appealing to all believers to seek after "Christlikeness," as God wants us to be "conformed to the image of his Son" (Romans 8:29). Christlikeness is the goal. That means you are to be the image of Christ in and to the world. Your life should reflect the values, manners, and mission of Jesus. What personal changes will make that goal a reality for you?

1. As disciples, we will go through a lifelong process of change. It is not a change that fades but one that increases and becomes more like the image of Christ. The plan is for you to be "changed into the same image from glory to glory, even as by the Spirit of the Lord" (2 Corinthians 3:18). The change takes place by abiding in the presence of the Holy Spirit.

2. For Christians, the peace of Christ must "rule in our hearts" (Colossians 3:15). Our hearts are restless and hostile without God's peace. This is especially true when there is discord or unrest in our relationships with others. We need the peace of God to act like an umpire that makes decisions in a heated contest. When the peace of God rules our hearts and mind it fosters harmony in our relationships. God's peace changes our attitude from bitterness and anger to harmony and love.

3. You should also give the Word of God room to dwell richly in our hearts (Colossians 3:16). We must give the Word of Christ plenty of room to guide our choices, actions, and word, so that we can become a more loving and forgiving believer. The Word renews our mind in righteousness and truth (Ephesians 4:23-24). The Holy Spirit is working in us to create a renewed attitude toward all of life.

4. Finally, you must align your life with the purposes of God. There should not be disharmony between God's purposes and your life's passion and mission. God is working to fulfill His mission in creation. He wants to use you as a believer to reach others, serve others, and to make a difference in your families, community, and nation.

To what extent can you expect these changes to happen in this life? It all depends on you abiding in the Spirit. The ideals above should become part of our spiritual desires. We should never lose sight of the fact that discipleship is a process of growth and change.

Summary and Life Application

Answering the call to discipleship will take a personal response and effort. This process does not end after baptism and membership in the church. Being a disciple of Jesus is a lifestyle. You should see the fruit of peace in your relationships, display love, and forgiveness, and be in complete obedience to God. These ideals are not beyond God's ability to help you achieve them. With God's help, you will make it. Remember, the moment you trusted in Jesus, you answered the call to complete love for God and others and to live in obedience to the Word of God. You are a disciple—a follower of Jesus. In fact, God wants your commitment and devotion to Christ to be rock solid and deep.

Remember these four principles:

1. Your goal in life is to become like Jesus Christ.
2. Make a bold effort to grow in the grace and knowledge of our Lord Jesus Christ.
3. Pray for the church that it succeeds at making more disciples like you.
4. Live a pure life and use your strength and resources to do good deeds in the world.

LESSON 3— WEEKLY ASSIGNMENT

Complete the questions below:

1. Where in the Bible can we find "the Great Commission?"
   ____
   ____

2. Write out the Great Commission below:

____

____

____

3. Take a moment to reflect on the following words of Jesus to His disciples, "If any man will come after me, let him deny himself, and take up his cross, and follow me" (Matthew 16:24).

4. Memorize the following passage: John 15:10.

5. List two areas of Christlikeness you believe God wants you to develop.

   a. ____________________________________

   ____

   b. ____________________________________

   ____

PRAYER FOR THE WEEK

Lord, please help me to put off the old man with all its sinful habits. Make my life a new life from the inside out, that I might become more Christlike. Renew my mind with peace and love. Help me to be the agent of peace in my relationships. Let your light shine through me every day. Help me to always be ready to do good works, in Jesus name. Amen.

LESSON 4

Growing Closer to God

Scripture: Psalm 73:28; James 4:8
Central Point: *God created you to have fellowship with Him and desires a closeness with you.*

Introduction

The life of a disciple of Jesus is more than a position or fulfilling a set of duties. When God calls us to Himself, He expects us to enter into a personal and growing relationship with Him. Discipleship is a life of *growing intimacy* with God. What does it mean to grow closer to God? By "growing closer," we mean developing fellowship or harmony with God. The opposite of growing closer is to be at odds with God. Certainly, that is not what God wants. A growing relationship with God is based on hands-on experience.

Knowing God Personally

Our relationship with God is personal. God is a personal being. We must understand that knowing God is not an optional part of our new life; it is the Christian life. Jesus said, "And this is life eternal, that they might know thee the only true God, and Jesus Christ, whom thou hast sent" (John 17:3).

The word *know* means experiential knowledge, not simply a knowledge of facts about God. It means to experience God's character. It is helpful to consider your relationship with God as an "I-God" relationship—between you and God. No one, but you, can live your life for God.

To know God more doesn't happen overnight. Just as it takes time to understand our friends, it also takes time to know God. The deepest desire of a Christian should be, "Oh, for a closer walk with Thee!" Jesus makes it clear that you should "Abide in me, and I in you "(John 15:4).

The call to know God personally runs throughout the Bible. The Psalmist said, "It is good for me to draw near to God" (Psalm 73:28). Remember, this relationship is mutual. The biblical promise to believers is if you "Draw near to God, and He will draw near to you" (James 4:8).

God wants you to know Him

What makes knowing God interesting is the idea that God wants to be known. The God of the Bible is the Supreme Ruler of all creation. All glory, majesty, and power belong to Him. Yet, while He is Supreme in power and status, God is a very personal God, and He wants to be close to you.

God's desire for personal fellowship with people is mentioned approximately eighty-eight times in the Bible. The Lord declares to Israel, "And you shall know that I am God" (Exodus 6:7). God's character is knowable. He wants you to know His will, ways, and nature.

The Lord will help you to gain knowledge about Him. In Jeremiah 24:7 God promised, "I will give them a heart to know that I am the Lord, and they shall be my people and I will be their God…" God graciously gave us a heart to desire and search after knowledge of Him.

It must be the desire of our hearts to grow in intimacy with God. This is an invitation to a personal and deep-seated spiritual trust in God. It is an intimacy that flows naturally from your spirit and soul. Remember, God is not an unknowable abstract idea or force; he is a personal living being. Although God is Supreme in power and status, He is remarkably personal and wants to be close to you.

How to grow closer to God

As a new and growing believer, you will spend the rest of your life maturing and deepening your relationship with God. Here are a few practical ways of growing closer to God.

1. Respect God's purpose for your life. Author Rick Warren, writing about God's purpose for human life, says, "You were created for God's pleasure." This means your life has a divine purpose. You must value this purpose (read Colossians 1: 16). God made you in his image. In Genesis 1:26 God says, "let us make man in our image, according to our likeness." Being made in God's image means we have some features and characteristics that God has.

2. Embrace fellowship with God. Revelation 4:11 says that God is worthy of all praise and honor, because He "hast created all things, and for thy pleasure, they are and were created." God delights in having fellowship with you. Your very existence brings God pleasure. God is your creator. When you recognize this truth, it will help you to see that your life is God's doing. Your life is not a coincidence. God's design for you is to be in fellowship with you.

3. Learn how to communicate with God through prayer. The Bible compares the "prayers of the saints" with sweet-smelling incense. Prayer pleases God. What is prayer? Prayer is a personal conversation with God. Prayer is an essential means to help you grow closer to God. Prayer helps us to seek God's will. Through prayer we seek "first God's kingdom and his righteousness" (Matthew 6:33). Prayer helps us to make God's will our first priority.

   Prayer is the means through which we confess our sins. When we pray, we show our dependence on God. We seek His forgiveness and His tender mercies during times of prayer. Psalm 86:1-7 is a prayer for God's preservation, mercy, forgiveness, and help in a time of trouble. Prayer releases spiritual power in your life. Paul prayed for the Ephesians that "according to the riches of his glory, he may grant that you may be strengthened in your inner being with power through his Spirit "(Ephesians 3:16). Every Christian should cultivate a habit of regular prayer. Praying regularly is an excellent way of strengthening our daily fellowship with God, as we confess our sins and seek His power.

4. Read the Bible regularly. The Bible is God's revelation to all humanity. The Bible can make us wise unto salvation. 2 Timothy 3:16 explains, "All scripture is inspired by God and is useful for teaching, for reproof, for correction, and for training in righteousness." Believers are "people of the Book."

   Joshua 1:8 says "This book of the law shall not depart out of thy mouth. You shall meditate on it day and night, so that you may be careful to act in accordance with all that is written in it: for then you shall make your way prosperous, and then you shall be successful." We read the Bible to grow in obedience. The promise to those who read and obey God's word is life of success.

5. Walk daily with Him. The word walk refers to a way of life, not merely the physical activity of taking stroll. People who walk with God tend to grow in their relationship with God. Walking with God means having His companionship in life. God accompanies us, and His presence gives us daily confidence. Deuteronomy 31:6 says, "for the Lord thy God, he it is that doth go with thee; he will not fail thee, nor forsake thee."

   To walk with God is to live in the Spirit. The Holy Spirit is God's presence that dwells within our hearts. Galatians 5:16 states, "Walk by the Spirit, and you shall not fulfill the lust of the flesh." God gives us the Holy Spirit to help us overcome the desires of the flesh. Walking with God means you agree with His ways. This means you can walk in God's ways in the choices you make and in the paths you choose. Never leave God behind.

6. Keep your distance from evil. Righteous people choose their activities carefully because they know that the ways of sinful companions can lead them astray. Romans 13:14 admonishes believers not to seek

opportunities to sin but to "put on the Lord Jesus Christ, and make no provision for the flesh, to gratify its desires."

Proverbs 1:10 cautions believers against following others to commit sin. The verse advises us, "if sinners entice thee, consent thou not." Christians must always reject the invitation to sin, no matter the promises. Sin is the tempter's snare. You have a personal duty not to seek an opportunity to sin or contemplate a scheme to sin.

Summary and Life Application

The life of a disciple is all about maintaining and growing a personal relationship with God. That's your number one goal. No other person can live the Christian life on your behalf. The level of intimacy you develop with God is your responsibility. Have you seriously thought about this calling? Why is this life so personal? It is because God wants you to know His character and will for yourself. He is a personal God who wants to have fellowship with you. Commit yourself to the task of growing closer to God by recognizing He created you for His pleasure. Spend time in prayer, seeking God's will for your life, and reading your Bible. Studying the Bible gives you the wisdom you need to grow in your knowledge of, love for, and relationship with God. Be conscious that God is a present companion with you as you make choices and live daily. Other Christians are on this journey with you. Further, reject all invitations to sin and never seek out ways of sinning against God.

1. How do you feel knowing that you were created to have fellowship with the Lord?

2. Are there other ways you can think of to help you grow closer to God?

LESSON 4— WEEKLY ASSIGNMENT

Complete the questions below before the next session.

1. What is the promise Jesus made in John 15:7 to those who abide in Him?

2. Why do you think Jesus wants you to "abide in Him?"

3. What two things can you start doing to draw closer to God?

a.

b.

4. How do you think your life will change as you grow closer to God?

PRAYER FOR THE WEEK

Great Lord, my deepest desire is to walk closer with You. I believe you created me to have fellowship with You. Help me to get to know You more as I read the Bible and pray. Give me wisdom to walk in the Spirit and to choose my friends and actions carefully, so that my heart will lovingly cling to You in obedience. Amen.

LESSON 5

Your Devotional Life

Scripture: Isaiah 26:9; Mark 1:35
Central Point: *Personal devotions are an excellent way to enrich your Christian life.*

Introduction

Welcome to another lesson in this series of studies. The objective to this point has been to help you better understand the life of the new disciple of Jesus. In our last lesson, we spoke about growing in your relationship with God. This lesson is a continuation of the previous lesson. Here, the focus is to provide you with a practical way of devoting yourself to God. In this lesson, you will learn how to carry out personal devotions. At this point in your journey with God as a new believer, it is essential that you lay the proper foundation for the life ahead of you. If you practice a regular pattern of personal devotions, you will set the tone of growth for your life as a Christian.

Personal Devotions

Personal devotion has to do with time set apart to spend time with God. It is a private and undisturbed time with God. Spending time with God is an integral part of deepening your relationship with Him. Personal devotions can be a powerful tool to inspire your soul, increase your desire to seek after God, and help you learn the principles of righteousness.

Personal devotion is a reflection of inner righteousness. Isaiah 26:9 expresses the prophet's personal desire to seek the Lord; "My soul yearns for you in the night my spirit within me earnestly seeks you. For when your judgments are in the earth, the inhabitants of the world learn righteousness." A righteous lifestyle is marked by a longing to know God personally.

Personal devotion is a way of following the example of Jesus. Jesus observed a quiet time for prayer and meditation. He got up and went out at dawn to spend time alone in prayer. Mark 1:35 says, "In the morning, while it was still very dark, he got up and went out to a deserted place, and there he prayed." If Jesus practised personal devotions, then so should every child of God. It is a time of fellowship with God so there are various blessings in store as you practice and nurture your faith.

The benefits of personal Devotions

Personal devotions carry tremendous benefits for the believer. It is the time when you get to meet with God personally. When the corporate worship service ends and the preaching is over, it is your turn to commune with God. Personal encounters with God can uplift your life. You get to connect with God in your own way. You can talk with God in your own unique style and meditate on His Words at your own pace. This is a time for you to relate to God personally.

As you build this personal relationship, you get a chance to see where you stand spiritually. You can assess your own walk with God and note where you need to grow as an individual. The plan is for you to grow closer to God, building your spiritual maturity. Spiritual maturity is not a destination—it is a process of personal growth. The Christian life is a journey.

Through personal devotion, you receive direction from God for your life. Time spent in personal devotion deepens your faith and life. Christians who spend time with God for themselves and by themselves are more likely to grow spiritually than those who do not. Since personal devotion is a sacred time with God, you must prepare and take it seriously.

How to plan your devotional Time

Useful Materials: A Bible, a notebook, and a pen or computer/tablet.

A place: Select a quiet place where you are free from distractions. Turn off the TV, radio, and phones. Be serious about spending quality time with God.

Set a time: Choose a time that is best for you. Usually, the early morning is best because that is when you are most alert. Set aside about 20-30 minutes. If you can commit to one hour, that is good.

Work with a plan: Divide your devotional time wisely. Use the following format as a plan for your devotions:

1. Opening moments [5-7 mins.]

Offer praise and thanksgiving: begin with a time of thanksgiving and praise to God. Take some time to confess your sins. Search your life for sins you might have committed and seek God's forgiveness. Seek His pardon and cleansing through the Holy Spirit and in Jesus" name. Pray for God's guidance. Ask the Spirit to reveal God's Word to you as you prepare to meditate.

2. Reading, Meditation, and Prayer [15-20 mins.]

Use the following Bible reading and meditation guide based on the acronym **S.O.A.P.** It begins with Scripture reading and ends with prayer.

S—is for survey*:*

a. Choose only a few verses.
b. Read the verses carefully.
c. Look at the details.
d. Read prayerfully and depend on the Spirit for guidance.

O—is for observe:

a. focus on the verse that stands out to you.
b. Wait to see what words, feelings, or images rise in your heart and tug at your spirit from this verse.

A—is for apply*:*

a. Think about how this verse connects to your life.
b. Is there an encouragement, a promise, an instruction, a correction, a sin to avoid, or an example to follow in the verse?

Ask yourself these other questions:

a. What is this passage saying to me about God, the church, the world, or myself? What action is it asking me to take?
b. What am I seeing in this passage that will help me to focus on living for God?

P—is for prayer:

a. Wrap up your devotions with prayer.
b. Talk to God about what you read, present your requests, and pray for others.
c. Ensure you tell God exactly how you feel and what is on your mind.
d. Speak freely and openly to God.
e. Make your requests known to God in the name of Jesus Christ, have faith as you pray, and wait for God's answer to your requests.

See example below:

Date: ______________ **Passage**: John 14:1-4

S = Do not let your hearts be troubled. Believe in God, believe also in me.

O = God does not want me to be troubled or stressed. He wants me to be at peace. If I believe in God, I must also believe in Jesus.

A = God is teaching me to trust Him. I sometimes worry about things, but I must trust and fully believe in God.

P = Father, teach me to trust and fully believe in your every Word. I pray that you help me to lean on and trust you in every area of my life.

Summary and Life Application

Remember, at this point in your walk with God, you are laying the foundation for the kind of life God calls you to live. You cannot survive and flourish in the Christian life without a regular habit of personal devotions. As a righteous person, your soul should long for communion with God. If Jesus longed to spend time with God, so should you. You stand to benefit from practicing personal devotions. You will cultivate your spiritual life, grow in your faith, and overcome sin through your personal devotions. Always consider a plan as you set aside time to be with God. This time should be spent in prayer, reading, meditation, and obedient response.

LESSON 5 – WEEKLY ASSIGNMENT

Throughout this week, practice the **S.O.A.P** method for your devotions. Use it each day as you read and meditate on the Bible and spend some time praying. Over time, you will develop the skill and knowledge to manage your sacred moments with God wisely.

Use the blank box below for the first day, then use a book or a journal for the other days. This will be a week of prayer, study, and meditation to help you develop your devotional life.

Remember these points:

S – Write out the verse or phrase that jumps out at you. Do not just write "I love verse 4." Write out the entire verse.

O – Using your own words, write out what you believe God is trying to tell you through your selected verse. Do your best. It does not have to be perfect, only honest.

A – Answer this question: "How does this truth apply to my life?" Think about it, and then write down what you believe God wants you to put into practice. Be real about this section.

P – Close with prayer and ask God to help you put into practice the message of your passage.

Date: ____________________ **Passage:** ________________

S = ____

____

O = ____

____

A = ____

____

P = ____

____

LESSON 6

The Importance of Water Baptism

Scripture: Matthew 28:19; Acts 2:38
Central Point: *Baptism helps to unite us with God in Christ through the work of the Spirit.*

Introduction

Welcome to another exciting lesson. Today, our focus will be on water baptism. Water baptism is one of the ordinances of the church. An ordinance is a Christian practice that the church carries out in obedience to Jesus. An ordinance is closely related to sacrament, which is an outward sign of an inward of grace. In other words, the act of baptism (an outward sign) points to the gift of salvation (an inward grace). The church performs baptism because Jesus commanded the church to baptize all those who believe the gospel message. In this lesson, we will explore why baptism is essential, the requirements and conditions for baptism, and other teachings on the theme of baptism.

What is Baptism?

The word *baptism* literally means "to immerse or dip." *Immersion* in water is the scriptural method for baptism. Baptism also means to be identified with or committed to someone. It is the outward sign of our profession of repentance and salvation. Baptism is one of the first steps of discipleship.

Baptism illustrates the death, burial, and resurrection of Jesus. Baptism joins and identifies the believer to all that Christ has accomplished. The Apostle Paul teaches that when persons come to Christ, they die to their old life. When a believer is put under the water, it represents the death of their old life. That experience is similar to being buried. Then, just as Christ rose again from the dead, so the baptized person rises again from beneath the water to walk in newness of life (Romans 6:1-4).

It is an essential step of obedience in a believer's life as a disciple. Everyone who believes in Jesus should seek baptism. It is the next step after repentance and believing. In the order of salvation, baptism follows repentance. Acts 2:38 says, "Repent and be baptized every one of you in the name of Jesus Christ for the remission of sins, and ye shall receive the gift of the Holy Ghost." Mark 16:16 also says, "He that believeth and is baptized shall be saved; but he that believeth not shall be damned."

Baptism is the next step after spiritual believing and repentance. Water baptism is essential for all believers. It is our testimony that we are fully surrendered to Christ. Baptism is important, but is it necessary for salvation? Do you need to be baptized to be salved?

Baptism is a sign of Salvation

Many people wonder if baptism is compulsory to receive salvation. It is critical to note that baptism is not *absolutely* necessary to receive salvation. Faith alone in Jesus as Savior and Lord is sufficient to save us from the penalty of sin. The Bible is clear about the plan of salvation, "For by grace are ye saved through faith; and that not of yourselves: it is the gift of God" (Ephesians 2:8).

Baptism does not and cannot save us from sin. God saves us by faith alone, through grace alone. When we put our faith in Christ, God, by His own grace, saves us. So, remember this truth, salvation is an act of God's grace, based on your faith in and acceptance of Jesus the Savior.

The Word of God teaches that baptism is a sign of having received God's forgiveness through faith. All those who accept the message of the gospel should be baptized. We noted above that baptism follows believing and repentance. Baptism is a sign of obedience and faith, but water baptism does not save us without faith in Jesus.

It shows your readiness and willingness to follow the will of God, as revealed through Jesus Christ. Although baptism is not necessary to receive salvation, God requires it of those who believe in Jesus.

Why is baptism a Requirement?

God directs the church to baptize believers. It is God's will that every believer be baptized in water. While our salvation in Christ is not dependent upon the act of baptism, God requires it as an expression of faith and obedience to Christ. In Matthew 28: 19, Jesus commissioned his disciples to baptize all who believe. He said, "Go ye therefore, and teach all nations, baptizing them in the name of the Father, and of the Son, and of the Holy Ghost."

Baptism symbolizes our forgiveness and union with Christ. "For as many of you as have been baptized into Christ have put on Christ" (Galatians 3:27). Baptism leads to us being "clothed" in the virtues that God grants to followers of Jesus. Baptism is to follow the act of repentance. The Bible teaches, "Repent and be baptized every one of you in the name of Jesus Christ for the remission of sins, and you shall receive the gift of the Holy Ghost" (Acts 2:38).

Baptism is clearly not something to be taken lightly. We practice baptism because God requires it for all believers. Baptism is a sign of our faith and salvation. It logically follows repentance and is required for membership in the body of Christ.

What are the conditions for Baptism?

The Bible sets forth various conditions that must be met by a person who desires baptism. As far as the church knows, those who repent of their sin have taken the first step toward water baptism.

1. A person seeking baptism must first repent and confess their sins: In Acts 2:38, the Apostle Peter says, "Repent and be baptized every one of you in the name of Jesus Christ for the remission of sins and you shall receive the gift of the Holy Ghost." Another condition for baptism is personal acceptance of the Gospel message. In Mark 16:15-16 Jesus says, "Go ye into all the world, and preach the gospel to every creature. He that believeth and is baptized shall be saved."

2. Next, a person must believe that Jesus is Lord. A sincere acknowledgment of Jesus as Savior and Lord is essential to our salvation and baptism. "Arise and be baptized, and wash away thy sins, calling on the name of the Lord" (Acts 22:16). Calling on the Lord means recognizing Jesus as Lord.

A person failing to sincerely believe and confess Jesus as Lord should not be baptized. The Bible does not teach the baptism of unbelievers. If a person is unwilling to forsake a life of sin such a person does not meet the conditions for baptism. On the other hand, if a person has sincerely turned to God through faith in Jesus, that person should seek baptism.

A few more scriptures on Baptism

Water baptism holds a unique place in our salvation. While baptism on its own does not save us, we are not to ignore its place in the process of salvation. Every physically able believer ought to follow Jesus in water baptism. Let us look at a few more scriptures on baptism to learn more about what the Bible teaches on this practice.

1. Jesus modelled baptism for us. Jesus was baptized in River Jordan to fulfill all righteousness (Matthew 3:13-15). If Jesus was baptized, then so should all of us. Water and Spirit baptism are essentials for entering the Kingdom. Jesus said, "Except a man be born of water and of the Spirit, he cannot enter into the kingdom of God (John 3:5).

2. Baptism is necessary to be added to the church body. "Then they that gladly received his word were baptized: and the same day there were added unto them about three thousand souls" (Acts 2:41). Someone who is not baptized should not be added to the local church membership. Baptism is the only act commanded by the Father, Son, and Holy Spirit. We are baptized in the name of the Father, Son, and Holy Spirit (Matthew. 28:19).

3. Baptism is required of all believers regardless of sex, race, or economic status. The Bible clearly states, "they were baptized, both men and women" (Acts 8:12). Paul teaches in 1 Corinthians 12: 13,

"For by one Spirit are we all baptized into one body, whether we be Jews or Gentiles, whether we be bond or free; and have been all made to drink into one Spirit."

As we can see, baptism is a sacred spiritual activity. It holds a special place in the teachings of the Bible and in the life of believers. On the day Jesus was baptized, not only did he include Himself in this tradition, be He explains to John the Baptist (the prophet who baptized Jesus) that it "fulfills all righteousness" (Matthew 3:15). Jesus clearly accepted baptism as part of His own journey as the Savior of the world. It was true for Jesus; then surely, it must be true for us as his followers.

Summary and Life Application

Water baptism is a gracious provision of a gracious God. It holds a special place in the life of a Christian. It is the act of being immersed in water as God's way of symbolizing that we are washed and renewed by the Holy Spirit. Remember, baptism originated in the wisdom and authority of God. On its own, it does not save us. We are saved by grace through faith in Jesus. At the same time, we accept it as God's requirement for all believers. Baptism marks the reception of salvation and the beginning of our new life in Christ.

1. When you think about your faith in Jesus and your repentance, do you agree that you are willing and ready to follow Jesus in water baptism?

2. Do you face any personal obstacles to prevent you from following Jesus in water baptism?

LESSON 6—WEEKLY ASSIGNMENT

Spend some time reflecting on the importance of baptism. Thank God for calling you to a life of discipleship. Think of your baptism as a new beginning in your life—a new spiritual birth. Mark and remember the day and date of your baptism as your spiritual birthday. Invite your family and friends to attend your baptism so that they may rejoice with you.

LESSON 7

How to Share Your Life's Testimony

Scripture: Isaiah 12:4
Central Point: *Your testimony is your personal account of what the Lord has done in your life.*

Introduction

Welcome to the final lesson in stage one of your discipleship journey. It is the hope that at this point, you are feeling confident in your salvation. You have covered some of the basic themes of discipleship and principles to grow your relationship with God. In this lesson, you will learn how to share your life's testimony. This lesson will give you the tools to stand boldly and share with others what the Lord has done for you. Testimonies are an important part of the life of believers, and God often uses your story to inspire others to faith.

What is your life's Testimony?

Simply put, your life's testimony is the story of how God saved you and gave you a new life. At this point, this is the story of your conversion experience—of how God saved you. No one can deny your testimony. It is your personal experience and account of what God has done and is doing in you through Jesus Christ.

The Bible says in Isaiah 12:4 "Praise the LORD, call upon his name, declare his doings among the people, make mention that his name is exalted." This verse invites the righteous to declare to others the wondrous praise of the Lord, to mention His name, and joyfully speak of His wonderful works.

We are called to share our testimony. Sharing your testimony with others is a powerful way of declaring what God has done and how He has turned your life around. God can and wants to use your experience as a tool to inspire them and exalt His name.

The importance of your Testimony

God wants you to use your testimony to answer those curious about your hope in Jesus Christ. If someone asks you to explain your reason for having hope in Christ Jesus, be ready to share your testimony. Your testimony is a powerful explanation for the reason for your faith.

In 1 Peter 3:15 the word of God says to us, "be ready always to give an answer to every man that asketh you a reason of the hope that is in you with meekness and fear." Your life's testimony is also a powerful weapon and defense against the accuser, Satan. Revelation 12:11 states, "And they overcame him because of the blood of the Lamb and because of the Word of their testimony." God's people are made victorious over Satan through their testimony. Our victory comes not by physical strength but by a life wholly dedicated to Jesus.

What should be in your Testimony?

Is there a way to organize and plan your testimony? The way you plan to share your testimony is significant. An unplanned testimony can turn out to be a long and uninspiring story about your life. However, a carefully planned testimony can be a real blessing.

When sharing your testimony, focus on these three main areas: before, how, and since:

1. **Before**—start your testimony by telling what your life was like **before** you came Jesus. Who were you? "Before I met Jesus, I was..." Don't just say, "a sinner," be descriptive and share a little detail to help others connect with your story. What was lifelike for you? E.g., "I felt my life going downhill..." What other problems, emotions, needs, and situations were you dealing with before you met Christ?

2. **How**—share **how** you got to the point of conversion and faith in Jesus as your Savior. What was happening? What people, events, or problems led you to seek Christ? How did it happen? Was it a sermon, a song, or an experience that led you to faith in Christ? Why now and not before?

3. **Since**—End your testimony by saying what difference Christ has made in your life **since** you trusted in Him. What has God taught you since trusting in Jesus for salvation? How have your attitudes, thoughts, and conduct changed since then? What is your determination as a new believer?

Remember to stick to the plan. Your conversion to Christ is the main focus of your testimony. You don't need to share your entire life story. Be specific and honest. Don't exaggerate or over-dramatize your life. The simple truth is good enough. People are very good at spotting a phony testimony.

Summary and Life Application

God wants to say something through you. Your life is His message to the world. Even after you have been baptized, it is important that you use this same pattern to share your testimony. Not every person's story is the same. Some stories are more dramatic than others. Do not compare your life's message with someone else's. There is a place for every story. As you move forward, live in a manner that will protect the message of your life. Guard your testimony from condemnation. Be ready to tell others about your personal experience with Jesus Christ.

LESSON 7—WEEKLY ASSIGNMENT

Read Acts 22:1-22 to see an example of how the Apostle Paul shared his testimony. Take the week to think through your life's testimony and be ready to share it with the church community and the world. Each person will be given 3-5 minutes to share her/his story, using the before, how, and since plan.

Write out your testimony in the space below. To help build your confidence, you can share it with a family member, someone from the discipleship class, or a trusted friend. Think about it carefully as you write. Remember, it is your story, not someone else's.

My Life's Testimony

Before:

____

____

____

____

____

How:

____

____

____

____

____

Since:

____

____

____

____

STAGE TWO

Practical Disciplines

LESSON 8

The God of the Bible (Part 1)

Scripture: Psalm 5:11; 148:13

Central Point: *God reveals His name as a way of showing His desire for fellowship with us.*

Introduction

The more God's people came to know God in the Old Testament, the more names they gave Him. Did you know there are approximately one hundred names for God in the Bible? There is so much we can discover about God by knowing His names. The names and titles of God in the Bible teach us a lot about His character, work, and His relationship with us. Today we begin a series of studies you will spend the rest of your life applying. For the following two lessons, we will be exploring the topic "The God of the Bible." God is personal and wants to be known. God does not hide Himself from people; He is not secretive. In fact, He has revealed enough about Himself so that you can know and relate to Him in a personal way.

What does the Word "God" mean?

God's word refers to God as the One who is worthy of all praise, who in love freely created the world, who sustains and governs all things. Christians affirm that the God of the Bible is the true and living God.

There are other specific names and titles that we use to identify and address God. God, Himself often revealed these names. God has never been shy to name Himself and to be addressed by His name. Knowing these names can help to deepen our relationship with the God of the Bible.

Names and Titles

When we try to describe God, we often do so by using His names and titles. There is a difference between names and titles. A *name* is a term used to identify God. For instance, *Jehovah* is one of the divine names used to identify and distinguish the God of Israel. As a name, *Jehovah,* can stand alone to describe God. It is generally translated as LORD in the Old Testament (in capitals letters). One example of this is found in Exodus 6:2 "And God spake unto Moses, and said unto him, I am the LORD."

On the other hand, *titles* emphasize "specific *things* about Jehovah—they describe Him in specific ways." For example, *God Almighty* (El-Shaddai) emphasizes "God's might." The word *Almighty* tells us something about God—that He is strong. You can worship and address God in a personal way when you know His name and titles.

The Trinity

The Trinity is an essential teaching in Christianity. It means that God is one, yet three. This teaching is difficult to explain and understand, but you must know how to apply its meaning.

One of the Bible's supreme claims about God is "God is One." Deuteronomy 6:4 declares, "Hear, O Israel: The Lord our God is one Lord" (Jesus quoted it in Mark 12:29). Most believers understand this verse to claim God's nature, namely, that God is one. In other words, there is no other being in existence on earth that is comparable or superior to God, whose name is Jehovah.

The Trinity signifies that God is "One, yet three." The thought that God is three means that there is one God who eternally exists as three divine or co-equal persons, namely the Father, Son, and Holy Spirit. We do not mean God has three forms—like water, steam, and ice.

An example of the Trinity is found in Isaiah 48: 16; Matthew 3:13-17; 28:19; 1 Peter 1:2. Another example is 2 Corinthians 13:14, which says,

"The grace of the Lord Jesus Christ, and the love of God, and the communion of the Holy Ghost, be with you all."
When we say that the Father is God, the Son of God, and the Holy Spirit is God, we do not mean there are three gods as in 1 + 1 + 1 = 3, but instead, it is 1 + 1 + 1 = 1. How is this possible? God is three in person, but one in essence or character. Each member of the Godhead is equally divine, eternal, and entirely harmonious in purpose. God is a holy mystery, and we cannot fully describe God's being.

Names of God

Here, we will be explaining the famous names of God the Father, Son, and Holy Spirit. We will begin with names for God the Father:

1. Jehovah or Yahweh (meaning "He who lives"). Yahweh is the most sacred name of the Father. In Exodus 3:14, "God said unto Moses, **I Am That I Am**: Thus, shalt thou say unto the children of Israel, **I Am** hath sent me unto you" (see also Exodus 6:3). This name is the most holy name and gives the idea that God is everything we can possibly desire Him to be

2. Elohim (meaning "Creator, Judge of the universe, or Strong One"). This name is commonly written in the Bible as *God*. We find it first in Genesis 1:1, "In the beginning, God (Elohim) created the heavens and the earth." It means God is the Creator of the universe and the maker of human life. Elohim is God's first and last name in the Bible (Genesis 1:1; Revelation 22:19).

3. God the Father (meaning "He who gives life"). In Mark 14:36, Jesus prayed, "Abba, Father, everything is possible for you." We are all children of the Father. Everything we know about God flows from his fatherhood.

You are free to address God the Father by any of these names. God loves it when you call Him by His name. The Bible teaches us that name of the Lord is righteous and a strong tower. Knowing God's name builds intimacy with Him. You will learn more of God's names as time progresses.

Names for God the Son

There are some 200 names in the Bible for God the Son. "Jesus" is the most used name for God the Son. Jesus is God's son in the sense that "He became flesh and dwelt among us" as the Son of God (John 1:14). The name Jesus means "God saves." It is given because He saves people from their sin.

Let us observe other important names for God the Son:

1. Son of God: This name highlights Jesus" position in the Trinity as God the Son. An angel told Mary, your child "shall be called the Son of God" (Luke 1:35). Jesus was asked, ""Are You the Son of God?" and He replied, "Yes, I am.'" (Luke 22:70).

2. Savior: This title speaks of his work of salvation. Jesus was sent into the world to be the Savior of the world (John 3:17). He is referred to as our "great God and Savior" in Titus 2:13. The angels announced, "To you is born this day in the city of David, a Savior, who is Christ the Lord" (Luke 2:11). This description of Jesus tells us exactly who He is—Savior of the World.

3. Christ: (Messiah or Anointed One). Jesus said, "The Spirit of the Lord is upon me, because he has anointed me to preach the gospel to the poor…" Luke 4:18. These two titles cover three aspects of Jesus" mission as King, Priest, and Prophet: (a) as *King*: He has "all power in heaven and on earth" (Matthew 28:18); (b) as *Priest:* He shed his blood to save us, and is "our intercessor" (Hebrews 7:25); and (3) as Prophet: He called on people to return to God (Matthew 21:11).

The name of *Jesus Christ* is wonderful. The name of Jesus is powerful to save anyone who believes in Him. The name of Jesus is precious to all Christians. You should cherish it as a treasure.

Names for God the Holy Spirit

We can learn about the Holy Spirit's nature and character through his names.

1. The Spirit of God: This name means "wind" or "breath of God." The Spirit of God is the life-giving power of God. Job 33:4 says, "The spirit of God hath made me, and the breath of the Almighty hath given me life." God is the living Spirit who gives us new life (John 3:6-8; 4:24).

2. The Holy Spirit: This name reveals the Spirit's role as the life-giver. The Spirit has a personality and can be grieved by us. "And grieve not the holy Spirit of God, whereby ye are sealed unto the day of redemption" (Ephesians 4:30). A life of sin can cause the Spirit divine pain.

3. The Counsellor: Jesus promises to send "the Counsellor, the Spirit of truth" to his disciples (John 15:25-26; 16:7). As our Counsellor, the Spirit guides us into doing the will of God.

In other instances, the Spirit is called "Spirit of fire" (Isaiah 4:4); "Spirit of Holiness" (Romans 1:4), and "Holy Ghost" (Acts 1:8). The Spirit walks by our side, gives us power, and stands with us in life. It is important that you trust in the Spirit's guidance as you live for the glory of God.

Summary and Life Application

Knowing the names of God should allow you to address God by name confidently. God reveals His name as a way of showing His closeness to us. The Psalmist says, "Let them praise the name of the LORD, for His name alone is exalted; His glory is above the earth and heaven" (148:13). Our God exists as Father, Son, and Holy Spirit. The Father is the powerful Creator and Sustainer of all life—including yours. The Father has the power to keep your life as you commit it to Him. The Son, Jesus, brought salvation to humanity and gives us access to God. Jesus made your salvation possible. Through Jesus, you can come boldly before God's throne of grace. The Spirit is the presence of God with us when we gather together or are apart. The Spirit of God is always with you. He promises "never to leave you, never to leave you alone," as the Christian hymn says. Be bold as you worship and call on the name of the Lord. Honor and love the name of the Lord.

LESSON 8—WEEKLY ASSIGNMENT

Search the Bible for other names of God.

1.The Father (Read Deuteronomy 32:8; Ecclesiastes 12:1):

____

____

2.The Son (Read Romans 11:26; Revelation 5:5):

____

____

3.The Holy Spirit (Read Isaiah 11:2):

____

____

PERSONAL DEVOTIONAL TIME

Spend 20 minutes in praise and prayer. Think about what these names mean and use them in your prayer. Use the name of Jesus in all your prayers as you ask God for His grace and blessings. Christians tend to end their prayer by saying "in Jesus" name." Depend on the Spirit to guide you in your prayer. The Spirit helps us to pray when we do not know what to say to God.

LESSON 9

The God of the Bible (Part 2)

Scripture: Exodus 34: 5-7
Central Point: *God is eternal in His nature and He is truthful, good, loving, and holy in character.*

Introduction

Welcome to the second lesson in this two-part study on the God of the Bible. In our last lesson we explored the different names of God. Today, we will be learning about the nature and character of God. The nature of God speaks to those innate or essential and unchangeable qualities of God. Character has a slightly different meaning. When speaking about God, character alludes to those traits that help us to understand God's personality. Why are these subjects important at this point? The simple reason is that the intimate relationship that believers enjoy with God produces grace and peace. 2 Peter 1:2 says, "Grace and peace be multiplied unto you through the knowledge of God, and of Jesus our Lord." Knowing God's nature and character can help us not only to honor and emulate His qualities but knowing God intimately is a means of grace for all believers.

The nature of God

When we speak of God's nature, we are talking about *what* God is in His being. Let us explore four aspects of God's nature:

1. God is eternal. The word *eternal* means having no beginning or end. God is completely timeless; He was never born and will never die. God lives forever! God existed before the world came into being. Psalm 90:2 declares that truth, "Before the mountains were brought forth, or ever thou hadst formed the earth and the world, even from everlasting to everlasting, thou art God." There is no past and future with God. "With the Lord, one day is as a thousand years and a

thousand years as one day" (2 Peter 3:8). The heavens and earth will pass away, but God lives forever. Jesus said, "Before Abraham was born, I AM" (John 8:58).

2. God is unchanging. God's nature is permanent and will always be the same. We read in Psalm 102: 26-27 that everything else will change and is subject to change, "But you remain the same, and your years will never end." God is consistent in His being. God cannot become something other than what He already is: "I am the Lord, I change not" (Malachi. 3:6).

3. God is Spirit. The Bible says, "God is a spirit" (John 4:24). God does not have any physical parts as we do. He does not share the same bodily life as human beings. God is a Spiritual Being. He is invisible. In Colossians 1:15, Paul called Him "the invisible God." As Spirit, God is hidden from our eyes, but He is present with us in our experiences. According to Paul, God is "immortal, invisible, the only wise God" (1 Timothy 1:17). Similarly, the Bible teaches that "God is light" (1 John 1:5). Here, John is implying that God is perfect; there is no evil in him.

4. God is all wise. Elihu, one of Job's friends, said God is the one "who is perfect in knowledge" (Job 37:16). The Apostle John declares that God "knows everything" (1 John 3:20). Paul also called Him "the only wise God" (Romans 16:27). God knows everything about everything. He does not lack knowledge or understanding on any matter.

When you think about what God is like, remember these points. The nature of God is His essence or substance. God is eternal; He outlives everything and everyone. God's purposes will not change. "The counsel of the LORD stands forever, the thoughts of his heart to all generations" (Psalm 33:11). God does not change with time. The fact that God is unchanging means you can rely on His steadfast character. God is all knowing. When you face life's uncertainties, remember God wants you to trust His unchanging character and wisdom. He can help you to find your way in life's darkest moments.

The character of God

The nature of God is *what* God is, but the character deals with *who* God is in His being. When you know who God is, it empowers you to model His character. God's character is praiseworthy.

1. God is truthful. This means that God is reliable when He speaks. When God speaks, He only speaks the truth. God possesses stability of character and a trustworthy nature. Deuteronomy 32:4 depicts God as a Rock and a God of truth. "He is the Rock, his work is perfect: for all his ways are judgment: a God of truth and without iniquity, just and right is he." God is the standard of truth, and there is no falsehood in God. Psalm 119:151 says all God's commandments are true, not lies. He delights in the truth and only speaks the truth. As Christians, we should love and speak the truth in love always.

2. God is good. All of God's actions are morally good. When we say "God is good" we are talking about His perfection and excellence. Exodus 34:6 says, "The LORD, the LORD God, merciful and gracious, longsuffering, and abundant in goodness and truth." God has an infinitely generous attitude toward you. Psalm 145:9 has this to say about the goodness of God, "The Lord is good to all, and his compassion is over all that he has made."

3. God is love. John tells us, "God is love" (1 John 4:8). This means that He eternally gives of Himself for the benefit of others. The love of God is not just about how He feels about people but who He is in character. God's character is one of pure love and not one of hatred. God loves mankind. "In this is love, not that we loved God but that he loved us and sent his Son to be the propitiation for our sins" (1 John 4:10). God loves us with an eternal love.

4. God is holy. The Bible calls God the "Holy One of Israel" (Psalm 71:22). Holiness means being separate from sin. God's holiness distinguishes Him from humans. He has no moral weaknesses and is perfect in all His ways. God hates sin and does not want us to sin. His word declares, "You shall be holy: for I the LORD your God am holy"

(Leviticus 19:2; 1 Peter 1:16). The Lord is holy, and He wants us to be holy in character and conduct.

When we think of who God is, we need to capture a big picture of all that He is. Our God is a God of truth, goodness, love, and holiness. These are virtues you should model in life.

Summary and Life Application

This lesson brings us to the end of a two-part study of the God of the Bible. Our view of God will have a significant impact on our respect for God. As Graham Kendrick said, "Worship is a response and will grow or shrink in direct proportion to our view of Him." So, as you grow in God, try to dig deeper in your knowledge of God. Learn more about His nature and character. Always show reverence for God. Trust in God because He is reliable. God never changes. Things and people will change, but God is steadfast. God created you to emulate His character. As a Christian, you should speak the truth in love, be good and do good to others, and love God and others and genuinely. Remember, holiness is God's standard of living for his people.

1. Knowing that God is eternal, how do you feel about approaching the future?

2. People and circumstances will change, but God does not. How can this build your confidence to face tomorrow?

LESSON 9—WEEKLY ASSIGNMENT

Use the rest of the week to read over these lessons until they are clear to you. In the process, take the time to get to know God personally, by name and character. As you pray, call upon the name of the Lord. Look at your life and see if you can discern God's love, goodness, and wisdom around you. Pray and ask God to help you relate to Him more thoroughly than before. Worship God and celebrate God for who He is.

LESSON 10

Resisting the Temptation to Sin

Scripture: James 1:13-15; 1 Corinthians 10:13
Central Point: *With God's help and grace we do not have to give in to temptation and sin.*

Introduction

It is a joy to have you on this journey once more. You are making significant progress, and the success of this discipleship program depends on your full participation. Today, we will be learning about temptation and how to resist the allurements to sin. Sin is breaking God's law. It is helpful to note that being tempted in itself is not a sin. It is yielding to the temptation that brings about sin. There are different sources of temptation, and God wants to help you recognize and resist temptation when it happens. At the end of this lesson, we will also explore various ways of resisting temptation.

The meaning of Temptation

Some Christians confuse the words testing and temptation. As you grow in Christian maturity and your ability to overcome sin, it is helpful to know the difference between these words. The word testing denotes the proving of our character or faithfulness to God. On the other hand, temptation means to entice or seduce to sin. Our focus will be on the word temptation.

Everyone has freedom of choice. In life, we often face instances where we are tempted to choose alternatives to God's will. Without such moments, there is no such thing as temptation or free will. So, on the one hand, temptation is due to our free will to obey or disobey God.

According to James 1:14, temptation comes not from God but from within us and our bending toward evil. The verse says, "But every man is tempted, when he is drawn away of his lust, and enticed." The source is internal, from one's lust. From the temptation to death, the progression of sin has an analogy in the physical life cycle: conception, birth, maturity, and death.

Yielding to temptation is Sin

God has nothing in His nature that makes sin appealing to Him. The Bible defines sin as breaking God's law: "Whosoever committeth sin transgresseth also the law: for sin is the transgression of the law" (1 John 3:4). Sin is disobedience or rebellion against God's will. It is also helpful to think of sin as missing the mark or falling short of doing what is right. "All have sinned and come short of the glory of God" (Romans 3:23). Sin when we give in to temptation.

God does not and will not tempt us to sin. "Let no man say when he is tempted, I am tempted of God: for God cannot be tempted with evil, neither tempteth he any man" (James 1:13). It is not a sin to be tempted; the sin lies in yielding. Remember, Satan himself cannot force you to sin; he can only allure you until he wins over your will. So, do not yield to temptation.

Sources of Temptation

The Bible reveals two primary sources of temptation: temptation by desire and temptation by Satan. Satan and our own desires can put pressure on our minds and emotions to sin against God. Both can be powerful and destructive forces if left unchecked.

1. Temptation by Satan. Satan is the enemy of God, and he uses seductive lies to cause people to sin. In Genesis 3:1-5 (Adam, Eve, and the serpent) and Matthew 4:1-11 (Jesus in the wilderness), we can see Satan's methods of tempting people. Satan tempts humans through seduction and deceit. The devil seduces people to oppose God's word and plans. He seeks to lead people astray from God's will by causing them to doubt or questioning God's word. Jesus said that Satan was a murderer and one who did not abide in the truth. In fact, there is no

truth in Satan, "when he speaketh a lie, he speaketh of his own: for he is a liar, and the father of it" (John 8:44).

2. Temptation by desire. While our natural desires are not sinful, they can become sources of evil in our lives. Our own human desires, or lusts, can be a source of temptation. James 1:14 says, "But every man is tempted, when he is drawn away of his own lust, and enticed." The guilt of temptation falls squarely on our desires.

We sin when we yield to Satan's temptation. Satan has no other agenda but to lead believers astray from doing God's will. Satan can also use our natural desires to entice us to sin. At other times, the source of our temptation starts within us. How can human desires become sources of temptation? When we do wrong for the sake of pleasure, when we seek comforts by giving in to our lusts, and when we lust for the vanities of the world. Temptation by desire often feels like "irresistible pressure" and entirely natural for you, but it has the power to draw your flesh into sin, away from God's will.

Consequences of yielding to Temptation

Yielding to temptation, either by Satan or desire, can harm our Christian life. Temptation leads to not only sin but also spiritual death and, often, physical death. James shows us the connection, "Then when lust hath conceived, it bringeth forth sin: and sin, when it is finished, bringeth forth death" (James 1:15).

In this verse, the Bible is very clear about what happens when we sin. Romans 6:23 says, "The wages of sin is death." There are real consequences for sin. Sin brings about intense guilt and shame. Sin separates us from fellowship with God and brings us under the judgment of God. When we sin, we compromise God's salvation in our lives and risk our own demise. However, the good news is that through God's grace, strength, and power, we can resist temptation.

How to resist Temptation

Temptation is mighty, but it is not almighty. God has put a limit on the intensity of temptations so that you can have a way to escape or overcome its strongest temptation. I Corinthians 10:13 says, "There hath no temptation taken you, but such as is common to man: but God is faithful, who will not suffer you to be tempted above that ye are able; but will with the temptation also make a way to escape, that ye may be able to bear it." With God's help, you can resist temptation.

7 habits to resist temptations:

1. "Watch and pray that you enter not into temptation" (Matthew 26:41). Do not think or live as though you are beyond temptations, but guard against Satan. Satan is a crafty enemy and is always at work to cause you to sin. Prayer helps you to escape temptation's traps.

2. "Resist the devil, and he will flee from you" (James 4:7). Satan cannot cause you to sin. You withstand Satan through a life of prayer, holiness, and submission to God's will.

3. Flee evil desires. We are to literally *run away* from settings that put pressure on our desires to sin. The Bible says, "Flee also youthful lusts: but follow righteousness, faith, charity, peace, with them that call on the Lord out of a pure heart" (2 Timothy 2:22).

4. Fill your mind with God's Word. The Word in Psalm 119:11, "Thy word have I hid in mine heart, that I might not sin against thee." Your heart and mind should be centered on the Word.

5. Know your weakness. Not everyone is tempted the same way. We are tempted by our own lusts, or desires. If you know your weakness, you can better resist the urge to yield.

6. Avoid companions who entice you to sin. Learn to say NO! "My child, if sinners entice you, do not consent." (Proverbs. 1:10).

7. Yield to God's righteousness. Romans 6:13 says do not "yield ye your members as instruments of unrighteousness unto sin: but yield yourselves unto God, as those that are alive from the dead, and your members as instruments of righteousness unto God."

Summary and Life Application

Sin and temptation can seriously affect your relationship with God. It is yielding to the temptation that is sinful. Guard against Satan and your own desires from drawing you away from God's path. Remember, do not trust your own human strength to resist temptation. It is unwise to refuse or hinder God's grace to help us during times of temptation. Let God help you through a life of prayer, daily submission, active resistance, and yielding to His righteousness. Without God's grace in a time of temptation, we are doomed to fail. Grace here speaks of God's strength and power released in us to help us overcome temptations. The first very of the beloved Christian Hymn *Yield Not to Temptation* puts it nicely.

Yield not to temptation, for yielding, is sin
Each victory will help you or some others to win,
Fight manfully onward, dark passions subdue
Look ever to Jesus, and He'll carry you through.

~Horatio R. Palmer

1. What is the difference between testing and temptation?
2. Explain the difference between temptation by Satan and temptation by desire?

If you have yielded to temptation, *confess to God.* Take a minute and talk with God. He knows about your sin. Tell God the truth about your failures and ask for His forgiveness.

Moment of *group prayer:* hold the hand of the person beside you and pray together. Ask God to give that person the strength to resist temptations by Satan and by their own desires.

LESSON 10—WEEKLY ASSIGNMENT

Memorize these victory verses: 1 Corinthians 10:13, 1 John 4:4, and Philippians 4:13.
Reflect and think about an area in your life where you are facing a temptation to sin. What are you tempted to do?

Write a prayer to God telling Him what you are facing and seek His grace for help:

____

____

____

____

____

____

____

____

LESSON 11

Knowing the Bible

Scripture: 1 Peter 1:20-21; 2 Timothy 3:16
Central Point: *The Bible is the inspired Word of God.*

Introduction

Welcome to another exciting lesson. Today's lesson is about knowing the Bible. The Bible is God's Word to the world. There are many books written about religion, but the Bible is the only one that claims to be, and actually is, the Word of God. What do you know about the Bible? How many books are there in the Christian Bible? Why is reading the Bible important? The Bible came about as a result of the work of God's Spirit. It makes this claim, "*Thus saith the Lord,*" more than 3,000 times. There are other things about the Bible that you need to know.

Facts about the Bible

The Bible was written over a period of 1600 years by approximately 40 men. The time of writing was between 1500 BC (Before Christ) to AD 100 (in the year of the Lord). This makes the Bible one of the oldest books globally, yet it is completely reliable and relevant to life today.

The Bible contains 66 books shared between the Old and New Testaments. The Old Testament is made up of 39 books, originally written in the Hebrew language. There are 27 books in the New Testament; these books were written in Greek originally.

On average, the Bible is over 600,000 words long, has over 185 songs, and is one of the world's most read books. The Bible is historically accurate. Many discoveries in archaeology support the accuracy of the Bible.

The Old and New Testaments

The Old Testament records the history of God's interaction with Israel. It is a rich source of spiritual teachings drawn from Israel's experiences, lives, laws, ceremonies, wisdom sayings, and prophetic traditions. Turn to your Bible's content page to locate the names of the Old Testament books. You should memorize their names and locations. The books can be divided into different sections:

1. The Pentateuch: These are the first five books of the Bible, from Genesis to Deuteronomy. Moses and Joshua wrote these books. They contain the records of creation and God's dealings with Israel. They are also called the "Law of Moses."

2. The Historical Books: These are the books from Joshua to Esther. They were written to help us understand the history of Israel. They describe how the obedience and disobedience of God's people can either lead to blessings or curses.

3. The Poetic and Wisdom Books: These include books from Job to Song of Solomon. In them, we will find the wisdom to guide us in how to live with knowledge and understanding before God.

4. The Major Prophetic Books: These include those books from Isaiah to Daniel. They are called "major" because of the amount of writing, not because they are more important. God used prophets to reveal His will and help us understand what He has done and plans to do.

5. The Minor Prophetic Books: These include books from Hosea to Malachi. These other prophetic writings were directed to specific situations faced by Israel and Judah.

The New Testament is the second section of the Christian Bible. The New Testament records the life of Jesus and the early church, especially the activities and teachings of the Apostles of Jesus.

1. The Gospels: These include books from Matthew to John. The Gospels give us four different accounts of the birth, life, ministry, death, and resurrection of Jesus Christ. The Gospels reveal how Jesus was the promised Messiah of the Old Testament.

2. The History Book: The book of Acts records the history of Jesus" apostles, the birth of the Church, and its rapid growth. It is a book about the mission and activities of the early church.

3. The Pauline Epistles: These are the books from Romans to Philemon. The Apostle Paul wrote them. He wrote them as letters to specific churches. In them, he gives official Christian doctrines and practices for the church.

4. The General Epistles: These are letters from Hebrews to Jude. They are similar to the Pauline Epistles with additional teachings for members of the church.

5. The Prophecy Book: The book of Revelation presents several prophesies about the events that will occur in the end times. Revelation is a book of hope for Christians. It is the final book of the Christian Bible.

The entire Bible is God's Word. The Bible is fully inspired by the Spirit and is therefore helpful for spiritual growth. This is what the Apostle Paul says, "All scripture is given by inspiration of God, and is profitable for doctrine, for reproof, for correction, for instruction in righteousness: That the man of God may be perfect, thoroughly furnished unto all good works" (Tim. 3:16-17).

Why is reading the Bible Important?

Many Christians do not spend enough time reading the Bible. Christians should make it their priority to read and study God's word. There are practical benefits when we read the Word. Reading the Bible teaches us how to live holy lives and to be fruitful witnesses for God (Psalm 1:3). When we read the Bible, it actively destroys unhealthy attitudes from our lives (1 Peter 1:23).

The habitual reading of the Bible enables us to grow in the knowledge and grace of the Lord Jesus (1 Peter 2:2). Another important reason to read the Bible is that it helps us understand God's will for our present and future walk with Him (Luke 11:28).

Different versions of the Bible

Have you ever wondered why there are so many different versions of the Bible? What do you think about the variety of Bible versions available today? Which version do you like to use?

To help us to understand the Word of God better, Christians have translated the Bible into different languages and versions. Each version or translation was written at different times in history, and all are useful in improving the believers" insights into God's word. Here are some examples:

1. *The King James Version* (KJV) was authorized by King James I. It was translated from Latin to English by the Church of England in 1611. The KJV is well-known around the world.

2. *The New International Version* (NIV) was written by more than one hundred Bible scholars from The New York Bible Society in 1973. It is an easy-to-read translation of the Bible.

3. *The American Standard Version* (ASV) is a revision of the King James Version and was released in 1901. This version updated the language of the King James for easy reading.

4. The *New Revised Standard Version* (NRSV), which was published in 1989, has received the widest acclaim and broadest support from academics and church leaders of any modern English translation.

5. *Pastor Eugene H. Peterson translated the Message Bible* in 1993. It does not use regular verse number formats as other versions. This Bible was published for easy and enjoyable reading.

Are so many versions a sign of confusion? No! The different translations are there to help make the Bible more understandable and readable in our language without losing the meaning of the original writers. There are numerous other versions in multiple languages to help the church in its mission.

Summary and Life Application

The Bible is God's Word. It is a collection of Books and letters. It is divided into Old and New Testaments. In one way or the other, every book in the Bible points to Jesus, the Son of God. Knowing and reading the Bible can help you deepen your understanding of God and His will. All the translations of the Bible are there to allow us to engage the Word in contemporary English, without losing the essence of God's message to His people.

Below is a schedule with daily Bible readings for the next seven days. Follow the reading plan in the table. A plan divides passages into manageable portions. Plans can be yearly, monthly, weekly, or daily. Following a plan is valuable to develop a regular Bible reading habit.

Read the passages each day. Each passage is a guide to specific areas of focus. Reading your Bible each day will strengthen your knowledge, grow your faith, and deepen your life as a Christian. Also remember to meditate and pray. Spend enough time to allow the Word of God to dwell in your heart. Pray as the Spirit leads you. Then, put the message of the Bible into practice as you live your everyday life.

LESSON 11—WEEKLY ASSIGNMENT

Take it one day at a time. Do not read all the verses in one day. As you read, do not be in a rush. Enjoy the passages, be prayerful, and listen to the voice of God as He speaks to your heart.

You are free to invite a family or friend to take this journey with you. Let the Word of the Lord be a blessing to your heart.

DAY	SCRIPTURES	AREAS OF FOCUS
1	Genesis 1-2; Isaiah 40:28	Appreciate all creation and the God who made all things
2	Genesis 3; Romans 3:23	Get a glimpse of sin and its effects on our lives
3	Genesis 12:1-3; Ephesians 5;	Value the gift of salvation that comes by grace through faith
4	1 Corinthians 10:13; James 1:4-6	Recognize that temptation is real and learn how to avoid falling to its power
5	Matthew 28:19-20; 1 Peter 3:14-16	Build the courage to be on a mission and be ready to be a witness of your faith.
6	John 1-2; Revelation 21	Be confident about Jesus" coming and near return to make all things new.
7	2 Timothy 3:16-17	Remind yourself of the Bible's value to your growth in righteousness.

LESSON 12

Disciplines for Every Christian (Part 1)

Scripture: Romans 12: 1-2
Central Point: *The Christian life is grounded in practical living based on the Word of God.*

Introduction

The remaining lessons in this section will be based on what is referred to as the Practical Commitments, an official document of the Church of God. It outlines the moral responsibilities and disciplines that should set apart the Christian life. These commitments are applicable to the life of all Christians. There are seven Practical Commitments, each relating to a different aspect of our everyday life. They are to be used as a guide in our spiritual, social, moral, and family life. This lesson will cover the first two of these commitments: Spiritual Example and Moral Purity.

1. **Spiritual Example:** *We will demonstrate commitment to Christ through our spiritual discipline, loyalty, and stewardship.*

Spiritual disciplines are practices or habits of a healthy Christian life. They are disciplines found in the Bible, and their purpose is to promote growth among believers and commitment to Christ. We may practice these disciplines alone or as a group in times of worship.

a. Spiritual disciplines that promote our spiritual example

A life of prayer and worship. As we pray, we express our trust in God, the giver of all good things, and acknowledge our dependence on Him for daily direction (Matthew 6:5-15). Coupled with prayer is the practice of worship. Worship is a means of having communion with God. Our life of worship should include personal alone time with God and our public celebration with other saints.

The practice of fasting. We draw closer to God and discipline ourselves to submit to the control of the Spirit through times of personal and corporate fasting (Matthew 6:16-18). Fasting helps to build our spiritual strength, loose heavy burdens, seek healing and baptism of the Spirit, and is an effective weapon of intercession.

Regular Bible Reading. We enhance our own spiritual growth and prepare ourselves to help guide and instruct others in scriptural truths as we read and meditate on the word of God (Joshua 1:8). The more our knowledge of God's word increases, the stronger our faith becomes.

b. Our spiritual example includes our loyalty

We show our loyalty when we meet regularly. We show loyalty when we meet regularly with other Christians for the purpose of magnifying God. We accept Sunday as the Christian day of worship. As the Lord's day, Christians celebrate the resurrection of Christ on a Sunday (Matthew 28:1). It is a day of worship, fellowship, service, and teaching of the Scripture (Romans 14:5-6).

We show our loyalty by tithing. We display loyalty through our willingness to provide for the church's financial needs by the giving of tithes (Malachi 3:10; Matthew 23:23) and offerings (1 Corinthians 16:2; 2 Corinthians 8:1-24).

We show loyalty by our mutual submission. We display loyalty when we respect and submit to those whom the Lord Jesus has placed over us (1 Thessalonians 5:12-13). We show our loyalty by our avoidance of oath-bound societies. Oath-bound societies such as lodges appear to be spiritual in character, but they contradict Christian spirituality (2 Corinthians 6:14-18).

c. **Our spiritual example also includes Stewardship**

Christians display their stewardship by our prudent use of money. The Bible promotes a moderate life but prohibits luxurious living (Matthew 6:19-23). A godly life requires the wise use of our temporal blessings.

We display stewardship by our management of time. As good stewards, we are to make the most of our time (Ephesians 5:16). The Bible discourages the idle use of leisure time (2 Thessalonians 3:6-13).

In addition to time and money, *we display stewardship by the faithful use of our spiritual gifts.* All our work and play should honor the name of God (I Corinthians 10:31). As good stewards, we must fully use our spiritual gifts for the glory of God.

All believers are expected to be spiritual examples in their commitment to godly disciplines, loyalty to God, and stewardship of God-given resources. These practices promote church growth.

2. **Moral Purity:** *We will engage in activities that glorify God and are beneficial to our spiritual well-being.*

What do you think it means to be morally pure? Perhaps the simplest way to think about moral purity is to view it as having "innocence of conduct." The opposite of moral purity is moral guilt. What can you do to live a morally pure life?

a. **Live in a manner that glorifies God.**

We glorify God by living our life in the Spirit, avoiding sin, and being disciplined. Our body is a temple for the Spirit. The Spirit lives within our bodies, and we are to glorify God in our body (Corinthians 6:19-20). Our goal is to leave no room for sin. Our strategy is moral discipline.

We are to walk in the Spirit and not fulfill the lust of the flesh. Some examples of fleshly "behaviors that dishonor God are noted in Galatians 5:19-21: homosexuality, adultery, and worldly attitudes (hatred, envy, and jealousy). Christians must not practice corrupt communication (gossip and filthy words), stealing, murder, and witchcraft. The activities we engage in must benefit our spiritual life. Our bodies are holy. God expects us to preserve the purity and holiness of our bodies.

As Christians, we must monitor what we read, listen to, and watch. The literature we read, the programs we watch, and the music we listen to can profoundly affect how we feel, think, and behave. Christians should read, watch, and listen to content that encourages godly living. Literature, programs, and music that are worldly in content or pornographic in nature must be avoided.

In our world today, we are bombarded with images that test our character and moral purity. A Christian has to be vigilant. Entertainment that disrupts our fellowship with God is to be avoided and forsaken at all cost. Everything we do should benefit our spiritual wellbeing.

Summary and Life Application

Christian living is not hypothetical living. It is not a life imagined. The Christian life is real. It is grounded in reality and highly practical. Each Christian should seek to practice the disciplines of the faith and always live morally pure. The use of our time, energy, and resources should be characterized by those activities which edify us personally and the body of Christ. We live our lives and trust God that it will be an example of goodness and purity to others. This happens when we practice the disciplines of the faith. In this moment, how do you rate your commitment to Christ?

Loyalty to the body of Christ is also important for the strength and growth of the church. As a believer, you should commit yourself to the ministry and fellowship of the local church. We are to avoid places and practices which do not honor God. A Christian must not be a part of any entertainment that brings discredit to the Christian testimony. This commitment is not calling on us to reject our everyday life and shun the world completely. It is simply asking us to monitor our social activities and guard our spiritual life with all diligence.

1. Is there an area in any of the two commitments that will be challenging for you to follow? If so, what makes it difficult?

2. How do you think having moral purity will help you in your Christian life?

LESSON 12—WEEKLY ASSIGNMENT

1. Spend some time thinking about this: "How are you being a spiritual example to others at this time of your life?"

2. If there is an area of moral weakness in your life, spend some time in prayer confessing that area to God.

LESSON 13

Disciplines for Every Christian (Part 2)

Scripture: 2 Peter 1: 1-7
Central Point: *The Christian life is grounded in practical living based on the Word of God and sanctification.*

Introduction

It is a delight to return once more to this wonderful journey. As believers, we aspire to live a life of integrity and responsibility. Living with integrity means soundness by adhering to strong moral principles. Overall, integrity expresses the idea of honesty. Along with integrity, we should strive to build strong Christian families. A strong Christian family is one that lines up with biblical principles. God created the family as a unit comprising one man, one woman—his spouse—and by God's blessings, their offspring or adopted children. In this lesson, we will focus on the practical commitments of Personal Integrity and Family Responsibility.

1. **Personal Integrity:** *We encourage every Christian to live in a manner that inspires trust and confidence, bearing the fruit of the Spirit and seeking to manifest the character of Christ in all their behavior.*

The thought of personal integrity has to do with how a person acts or thinks concerning their values. Put another way; personal integrity is doing what you believe is right. Personal integrity inspires trust, cultivates the fruit of the Spirit, and reflects Christ.

a. Inspires trust and confidence

As a Christian, you should be trustworthy, dependable, and a person of your word. People should have confidence in your character. People should be able to trust your word. In Matthew 5:37, Jesus commands, "let your words be yes or no." For Jesus, you should not have to swear an oath to be trustworthy. A simple and honest "yes" or "no" should suffice. We should build trust in our relationships. Paul says, "Be kindly affectioned one to another with brotherly love; in honor preferring one another" (Romans 12:10). Honesty and kind affection can go a long way in building solid relationships based on trust and confidence. God will help you along the way.

b. Cultivates the fruit of the Spirit

In Galatians 5:16, we read, "This I say then, Walk in the Spirit, and ye shall not fulfill the lust of the flesh." Christian character is the result of fruit produced by the Spirit in our life. The Fruit of the Spirit has nine qualities that should govern our minds and conduct. They can be found in Galatians 5:22-25, and they are love, joy, peace, longsuffering, gentleness, goodness, faith, meekness, and temperance.

c. Reflects the character of Christ

Love for others is the hallmark of Christian character. Christ Jesus is our greatest example of sincere selfless love for others. Submission, acceptance, and compassion are signs of love. In His relationship with His Father, Jesus displayed submission (Luke 22:42). In His relationship with others, He demonstrated acceptance (John 8:11), compassion (Matthew 9:36), and forgiveness (Luke 5:20). We must follow Christ's example in our relationships and live by His principles. We cannot bear the fruit of the Spirit and manifest the character of Christ without abiding in Christ (John 15:4-5).

At this point in your life, do you honestly believe people can trust you? There is a crisis of trust in our world. This is true on every level of society, in homes, schools, government, and sometimes even among believers. Your life should be different. Christians should not compromise their integrity by cheating. Christians are promise keepers. Their words are honest, and they are not afraid of the truth. Their character is sound. Does that sound like you at this point? The Spirit does not cultivate these qualities in a believer's life overnight. You should allow the Holy Spirit to develop this character within you so that you can live a mature and Christlike life in the world.

2. **Family Responsibility:** *Each Christian should give priority to fulfill ling family responsibilities, preserving the sanctity of marriage, and maintaining divine order in the home.*

God created the family as the basic unit of human relationships. The family is foundational to the church and society. Given its divine origin, we must prioritize the family above any other form of social institution.

a. Practice of Christian disciplines in the home

In Deuteronomy 6:6-7, God instructed parents to teach the law to their children in the home. Prayer, thanksgiving, reading of scripture, love, kindness, goodness, and other virtues should start in the family. The family must be built on the principle of love. Without love, the family cannot grow and perfect itself as a pattern of God's will. All Christian families should practice family devotions and endeavor to provide a healthy environment in the home. Christian families should be a place of life, love, support, and prayer.

b. Honor the sanctity of marriage

Marriage is holy unto the Lord. Marriage is ordained of God and is a spiritual union between one man and one woman (Genesis 2:24; Mark 10:7). We believe marriage is to be a lifelong commitment with the only clear biblical allowance for divorce being fornication or adultery (Matthew 5:32; 19:9).

Sexual involvement before marriage or with someone other than the marriage partner is forbidden in Scripture (Exodus 20:14; 1 Corinthians 6:15-18). Should divorce occur, the church should be quick to provide love, understanding, and counsel. A single lifestyle is a viable alternative for divorced believers (1 Corinthians 7:8, 32-34).

c. Agree to the divine order in the home

When God created man, He created them male and female (Genesis 1:27). He gave us distinct characteristics (1 Corinthians 11: 14-15) and different responsibilities (Genesis 3:16-19). In God's order, the husband is head of the home (Ephesians 5:22-31; Colossians 3:18-19). The Christian husband does not control his wife but loves her and provides for the family's physical needs. He is to be responsible for the family. The wife is to love her husband and care for the physical needs of the family. She should choose to submit to the headship of her husband in love, not because of fear, or force. As parents, the husband and wife are to nurture and admonish their children in the Lord (Ephesians 6:4; Colossians 3:21). Children are to obey and honor their parents (Exodus 20:12; Ephesians 6:1-3).

For harmony to exist in the home, we encourage believers to observe God's order. This must be done in love and grace, not by fear, force, or physical and emotional control. Some individuals object to God's order. Usually, that is due to a lack of understanding.

Summary and Life Application

As Christians, personal integrity and family responsibility are signals of our growing relationship with God. People should trust your word and character. Your speech should be honest and straightforward. Do not swear to show how serious you are; a simple "yes" or "no" should suffice.

As you grow as a believer, seek to bring your family in line with God's will. If you are a parent, you share that role with your life's partner. If you are a child or teen, God expects you to be obedient.

1. At this point in your life, can other people rely on your word?
2. Why is it important that you make promises and keep them, especially to your family?
3. What do you make of God's plan that the husband is the leader of the family?

LESSON 13—WEEKLY ASSIGNMENT

Make this a **family** activity. Get everyone involved and ask them to be your monitor for the week. As much as it is possible follow the activities below:

1. Try and be completely honest with the members in your family for the course of this week (and beyond).

2. Show a genuine interest in the other members of your family. Be fully attentive to the lives of other family members, especially children or spouse. Honestly listen to them.

3. Spend 30 minutes in prayer as a family, allowing each member to take turns in prayer and Bible reading. Share your thoughts on the Bible readings.

LESSON 14

Disciplines for Every Christian (Part 3)

Scripture: 1 Peter 3:1-4
Central Point: *The Christian life is grounded in practical living based on the Word of God and sanctification.*

Introduction

Welcome to this final lesson in this three-part series on practical Christian living and in this section of our discipleship program. At this point, you would have completed thirteen exciting lessons. The hope is that by now, you are experiencing a steady growth in the Lord. This week is also a special week as, during this week, you will engage in seven days of fasting. Do not worry; you will not be doing it alone; the church community will join you. The fasting plan is simple and easy to manage. You will find the weekly schedule at the end of this lesson. As we bring this section to a close, we will learn about temperance and our social obligations. As Christians, we aspire to live by the principles of temperance, moderate living, and responsible social obligation.

1. **Behavioral Temperance:** *We will practice temperance in behavior and will abstain from activities and attitudes which are offensive to others, or which lead to addiction.*

One of the central Christian virtues is temperance or self-control. Temperance means restraint or moderation. The apostle Paul lists temperance as one of the fruit of the Spirit in Galatians 5:23.

a. **Practice moderation in our behavior**

Moderation is the middle ground between two extremes. It is non-excessive behavior. Moderation promotes self-discipline and reveals the power of God at work in our thoughts, speech, and conduct (1

Corinthians 9:27). A believer must live a life of discipline to avoid being judged as morally corrupt. Self-disciple is similar to behavioral temperance, which means to put a bridle on the natural passions of our flesh. As believers, we must control our thinking, our anger, and our communication.

As a Christian, do your best to avoid offensive behavior. In Matthew 22:39, Jesus says, "Love your neighbour as you love yourself." Loving our neighbour involves showing care and consideration to those who cross our paths. At times we must control our behavior so as not to bring offense to others.

b. **We should love and respect others**

Henri Nouwen, a Dutch Catholic Priest, once said that true community is the place where the individual, we least like always lives next door. Jesus commands his disciples: "Love one another; as I have loved you" (John 15:12). One way of expressing love is to have *forbearance,* which means being patient and respectful of others for God's sake. Love and respect are important elements in the language of godliness.

c. **We should live in freedom from addiction and enslavement**

One of the primary benefits of our liberty in Christ is freedom from the domination of opposing forces. Galatians 5:1 speaks of our freedom in Christ from the law, a "yoke of bondage." However, our spiritual freedom also implies physical liberty. We should not be slaves to anything. A Christian must seek to abstain from alcoholic beverages and abstain from other habit-forming and mood-altering substances such as tobacco, marijuana, and other addictive substances. Proverbs 20:1 state, "Wine is a mocker, strong drink is raging: and whosoever is deceived thereby is not wise."

Why do you think a Christian should not be given too much wine? We must refrain from gambling and other activities that can dominate our lives. Christ has made you completely free.

2. **Modest Appearance:** *We will demonstrate the scriptural principle of modesty by appearing and dressing in a manner that will enhance our Christian testimony and will avoid pride, elaborateness, or sensuality.*

We are living in a society that puts a lot of attention on fashion. Unfortunately, some Christians do not know how to draw the line between appropriate and inappropriate appearance. Let us talk about a few principles of Christian modesty.

a. **A Christian should live modestly**

What does modesty even look like? First, *modesty is an inner spiritual grace that withdraws from anything unseemly and impure*. It means to be chaste in thought and conduct and free of indecency in dress, speech, and conduct (Ephesians. 4:25-31). Modesty can be applied to all situations. Simply ask, "Is this pleasing or displeasing to God?"

Our character and self-image are reflected in our appearance. The scripture says, "Be not conformed to this world." (Romans 12:2). For both males and females, our manner of dress must be modest and decent, not loose and showy.

Reject pride, elaborateness, and sensuality. As godly people we are to abstain from all lusts of the flesh and avoid dressing in a manner that encourages an immoral lifestyle, which the Apostle Peter says, "war against the soul" (1 Peter 2:11). Our beauty does not depend on extravagance, costly attire, or the use of jewellery and cosmetics but our relationship with Christ. Whether clothing or jewellery, as an outward display of personal worth, the focus on external adornment is contrary to a spiritual attitude (James 2:1-4).

Do you think modest living means Christians should carry themselves in an untidy or unkempt manner? Certainly not. It is not displeasing to God for us to dress well and be well-groomed. However, our emphasis should not be merely on external appearance; we must seek spiritual beauty. Spiritual beauty does not come from outward adornments but good works, pure conversations, and a meek and quiet spirit.

3. **Social Obligation:** *It should be our objective to fulfill l our obligations to society by being good citizens, by correcting social injustices, and by protecting the sanctity of life.*

As Christians, we live in the social order of this world, and we are to act as responsible citizens. God has given believers a social obligation to promote peace globally by living as model citizens.

a. **Be good citizens**

Romans 13:1-7 teaches us that God has delegated some authority to human governments. For instance, the government helps to uphold order, provide jobs, and execute justice in our society. How must we understand this in our daily life? We should support civil law and order, hold our leaders in respect, pray for them, participate in schools, community, and governmental activities, exercise our voting rights, and defend moral issues. God's law is supreme, but we are to obey the laws of our country once they do not conflict with obedience to God (Acts 5:29).

b. **Work to correct social injustices**

God's love for all humankind should compel us to take steps to improve the situation of those who are underprivileged, neglected, and victimized (Matthew 22:39). We must be sensitive to human needs (Luke 10:30-37), guard against racial discrimination, economic, social class discrimination, and gender discrimination.

c. **Protect the sanctity of life**

God alone is the creator of life (Genesis 1:1-31); therefore, we are responsible to God to care for our physical lives and others. If the circumstances require, we must be prepared to risk our lives in the service of others (John 15:13). God alone confers life, so God alone must decide when it should end. A human fetus is sacred and blessed of God; we must protect the life of the unborn (Jeremiah 1:5). Abortion and euthanasia of the aged, mentally, and terminally ill, or otherwise handicapped are morally wrong for reasons of personal convenience. We must also stand up for environmental justice. In the beginning,

God gave man dominion over the earth (Gen. 1:26-30). This does not give us the license to pollute and waste our natural resources.

It is our Christian responsibility to care for people, the earth, and all its natural resources. A Christian should build their country and be a good citizen.

Summary and Life Application

It is helpful to remember that Christians live accountable lives morally, socially, and spiritually. We seek to live by self-control, limiting our freedoms and passions for the sake of Christ. We understand that what God looks at is our heart and not our outward appearance. However, this does not mean outward appearances are not necessary. A Christian should dress decently and in keeping with appropriate fashion. A Christian, however, emphasizes the beauty and purity of the inner character. All believers are to be good citizens. Each one must abide by the rule of law, pay their taxes, seek justice, and protect the environment.

Take a moment to reflect on what it means to have self-control when it comes to (1) our communication, (2) our relationships, and (3) using addictive substances. What about Christians and fashion? Should Christians be fashionable? Remember, the way we live as the people of God must never betray the values of the Christian faith. Our personal conduct and social responsibility are important ways of living for God's glory and being a testimony of God's power to change lives.

As we come to the end of this section, we must remember that the Christian life is practical. It is real living. That is why we believe that all believers should adhere to some basic form of practical commitment. If we do not commit, it is easy to fall for and adopt attitudes and "behaviors that do not honor God.

We have tried to show how the Bible speaks to every area of human life. However, we do not need to identify every single area of human life to know what God wants. The principles we learned in this section allow us to glimpse the core of Christian practice. If you put them into practice, your Christian life will grow.

LESSON 14—WEEKLY ASSIGNMENT

Do you have temperance and self-control over your desires and habits? One way of helping you is to put yourself to the test. This week we will undertake a significant activity that will test your self-control and spiritual discipline. We will spend one week in prayer and fasting.

Testing yourself control

1. Your eating: what foods can you eat less of this week?
2. Your anger: how can you be calmer this week?
3. Your entertainment: what can you limit your involvement in this week?
4. Your passions: what desires can you bring under control this week?

Building your Spiritual discipline

For this week, you will spend some time in prayer and fasting. You will follow the plan below. Remember, you are not doing this alone. The church community or one of the groups in the church will be on this fast with you. This plan might be intricate for a child or teenager who is currently in school. If that is your case, you might have to find a way to join the fast without risking your health and education. Speak with your discipleship member about this fast.

A final note; do not rush ahead of the plan. Pray one day at a time and pay attention to the prayer times, daily prayer focus, readings, and meal plan. This is not a race. Note that you will have an all-day fast on Wednesday. If your church has fasting on this day, you can join that fast. The plan is for you to feel that you are on a journey with other believers.

Fasting Plan and Focus

The following plan should last for one week only. Your goal is not to lose weight, but to build spiritual strength and develop the disciplines of fasting, prayer, and Bible reading.

<table>
<tr><th>Times</th><th>Day</th><th>Daily Prayer Focus</th><th>Daily Readings</th><th>Type of Fast and Meal Plan</th></tr>
<tr><td rowspan="6">Seeking the Lord

Prayer Times

Mornings: 6:00—6:30

Noon: 12:00–1:00

Nights: 9:00—9:30</td><td>1</td><td>Your Family: spouse, children, brothers and sisters, extended family, and neighbours for guidance and blessing.</td><td>Psalm 127:1-5; Acts 16: 31-34</td><td rowspan="6">Make a special effort to follow the prayer and meal plan for the week. This fast is a partial fast.

Skip Breakfast
Monday and Friday (1 cup sugarless tea is permitted)

ALL DAY FAST
Wednesday
6:00 am–5:30 p.m.

Skip Lunch
Tuesday and Thursday
No meat on Thursday.

Supper/Dinner
Eat light dinners. Fruits and vegetable are best. Sugarless tea permitted at nights. Drink water or no sugar natural juice at dinner.

NO SNACKING all week</td></tr>
<tr><td>2</td><td>Church Family: Pastor, church council, leaders, members of the church for daily guidance, power, vision, holiness.</td><td>1 Kings 8: 33-36; 1 Peter 5: 1-3;</td></tr>
<tr><td>3</td><td>Outreach: Effectiveness in witness, your ministry, your spiritual gifts, and prayer for specific non-Christians.</td><td>Isaiah 49:1-6; Acts 1:6-11</td></tr>
<tr><td>4</td><td>Spiritual Growth: For growth in grace, knowledge, to walk in the spirit, Christian character, hope, and victory over sin.</td><td>Proverbs 1:1-5; Ephesians 4:20-24</td></tr>
<tr><td>5</td><td>Authorities: government and opposition, police and security forces, all health workers, teachers, and employers for daily guidance.</td><td>Ezekiel 22: 29-31 1 Timothy 2: 1-2</td></tr>
<tr><td>6</td><td>Nations: Those experiencing fires, famine, war, turmoil, and who have never heard the gospel.</td><td>Select your reading for today</td></tr>
</table>

STAGE THREE

Core Beliefs

LESSON 15

The Purpose of the Church

Scripture: Matthew 16: 13-19; Acts 2:42-47
Central Point: *The church is God's plan to help believers grow in grace, knowledge, and service.*

Introduction

You have just entered the final stage of this program. You have come this far by faith and commitment. Take a moment to reflect on what the journey has been like for you. What significant experiences stand out to you? How was the week of fasting and prayer? What did you learn about yourself during the fasting? As you progress, you will notice yourself growing even more than you have already done. In this stage, you will learn about the purpose of the church, the Pentecostal movement, and various statements of faith for the Church of God.

What is the Church?

Evangelist, the late Billy Graham, explains it this way, "the church isn't just a particular building or congregation but the spiritual fellowship of all who belong to Jesus Christ." Simply put, the church is the body of "called out believers" who have trusted in Jesus Christ as Savior.

Jesus, the Messiah, is the founder of the church. In Matthew 16: 15-18, Jesus asks His disciples, "Who do you say that I am?" The disciple Peter answered, "You are the Christ, Son of the living God." In response to Peter's statement, Jesus declares, "Upon this rock, I will build my church." The church of Jesus is not simply the gathering of those who belong to a local congregation. Anyone can adhere to a local fellowship. The church is the spiritual body of believers who have been called out of the world to live a holy life, service, and obedience to God.

Paul writes in 1 Corinthians 1:2, "Unto the church of God, which is at Corinth, to them that are sanctified in Christ Jesus, called to be saints." The church is made up of people called out or separated from the world because of their relationship with Jesus. That means in Christ, we are made holy, separated unto God, and become church members.

Let us think about it another way. When you received Jesus as Savior, you were born again and given a new spiritual life. A new spiritual life is a key ingredient for your membership in the church.

The purpose of the Church

The Bible uses many descriptive terms to teach us about the purpose and identity of the church. There are more than eighty (80) descriptions of the church in the New Testament. For example, the church is described as the disciples of Christ (John 17:6-26), Christians (Acts 11:26), the God's household (Ephesians 2:10-19), the servants of righteousness (Romans 6:18), and many more.

Such rich descriptions are intended to help us grasp God's vision and intentions of who we are in Christ. All are valid and can help us understand the rich meaning of the church and why it exists. In a general sense, the ultimate purpose of the Church is to live *for*" the praise and glory of God" (Ephesians1:6, 12; Revelation 4:11). The church exists for God's pleasure, alone. How does the Church bring glory to God? We bring glory to God when we:

a. Worship God—for the church, worship is an expression of reverence and adoration of God for who He is and what He has done. We worship the Lord by expressing our love for Him individually and collectively as a body. Worship requires us to love the Lord with all our heart, soul, and mind (Matthew 22:37; Deuteronomy 6:5). We worship God in everything we do.

b. Evangelize the lost—the church fulfills evangelism by spreading the gospel to the lost (to unbelievers) through personal witnessing or public preaching. The Apostle Paul declared," For I am not ashamed of the gospel of Christ: for it is the power of God unto salvation to everyone that believeth; to the Jew first, and to the Greek (Romans 1:16). Sharing the gospel is not an option for believers but a central purpose and requirement for the church.

c. Fellowship with one another—the church fulfills fellowship by sharing love, spiritual graces, and suffering. Fellowship helps to build unity and devotion within the church (Acts 2:42). Paul says we "no more strangers and foreigners, but fellow citizens with the saints, and of the household of God" (Ephesians 2:19).

d. Disciple believers— discipleship is imitating the example of Christ. God calls the church to model the life of Christ in thoughts, feelings, and actions. Discipleship requires believers to respond to the Holy Spirit's work in their souls here on earth. The church plays a role in helping all believers to grow in faith, grace, and the knowledge of Christ. As disciples, we also develop our spiritual gifts in preparation for total service to God (Ephesians 4:11-13).

e. Minister to people—Ministry is exercising our spiritual gifts in service for the benefit of other people. God has called the church to be humble servants of Jesus Christ who must care for those in need (Acts 2:45). Every action we perform should be done as an act of ministry, enabled by God's Spirit, and energized by love and concern for the wellbeing of other people.

Your life as a Christian should bring glory to God. You can interpret the five purposes above to give your life meaning. As a Christian, you are a worshiper, evangelist, fellow believer, follower, and minister of Jesus Christ. Your character and purpose of life should reflect those purposes.

Why is church attendance Important?

Each time believers gather together, whether generally or in small groups (such as men, ladies, youth, or children) for prayer or Bible Studies, it is to fulfill a God-given purpose. People who regularly attend church are more likely to develop a richer understanding of the faith, live obediently to God's word, and serve as witnesses of the Gospel, than those who do not attend church regularly. This makes church attendance an important matter.

Here are some more reasons you should regularly attend church:

a. We attend church because it fulfills the command of God. Hebrews 10:25 says we should not forsake "the assembling of ourselves together, as the manner of some is but exhorting one another." The renowned evangelist Dwight L. Moody once said, "Church attendance is as vital to a disciple as a transfusion of rich healthy blood is to a sick man."

b. We attend church because it makes a difference in our spiritual lives. Church attendance helps us to develop spiritually. Romans 14:19 states, "Let us then pursue what makes for peace and for mutual upbuilding." God enriches your spiritual life when you listen to a sermon, participate in Bible study, sing songs, pray, give your offerings, and share in Holy Communion.

c. We attend church because it helps us to keep God as our priority. Matthew 6:33, "But seek ye first the kingdom of God, and his righteousness; and all these things shall be added unto you."

d. We attend church because it helps the congregation to grow. When you attend church frequently, it helps supply workers: song leaders, teachers, ushers, youth workers, and others. Your physical presence adds to and encourages an atmosphere of growth in the church.

As children of God, we need to have the same attitude expressed by the Psalmist, "I was glad when they said unto me, Let us go into the house of the Lord" (Psalm 122:1). Church membership and attendance matter and you should take your membership in the church seriously.

Summary and Life Application

The Bible teaches us that the church is the fellowship of believers who have been called out of the world by God. Simply being an adherent of a church does not equate to being sanctified in Jesus. We become members of the church through spiritual birth and not by affiliation. God created the church for a purpose, which is to live for the praise of His glory. Remember, the church is not a building; the church is the people of God. It therefore means, your character and purpose of life should be driven by the same purposes as the body of church. If you have not yet done so, make a firm commitment to attend church regularly. All believers must support the church. Attendance to church services is a powerful way of growing more robust in the grace and knowledge of Jesus. The Lord instructs us to establish and maintain a strong connection with fellow Christians.

LESSON 15—WEEKLY ASSIGNMENT

As a member of the body of Christ—the church—how do you think God is calling you to live in this world? Fill in the spaces.

1. As a *worshiper,* God wants me to

   ____

   ____

   ____

   ____

2. As a *witness* God wants me to

   ____

   ____

   ____

   ____

3. As a *fellow Christian,* God wants me to

____

____

____

____

4. As a *disciple,* God wants me to

____

____

____

____

5. As a *servant,* God wants me to

____

____

____

____

____

LESSON 16

The Pentecostal Movement

Scripture: Acts 2:1-4
Central Point: *Pentecostalism is a movement that believes in the direct personal experience of the Spirit.*

Introduction

Welcome to today's lesson. Our focus today will be on Pentecostalism. Pentecostalism is a spiritual movement within Christianity. It started when a group of Christians went on a quest to address questions about their salvation. One of the questions that inspired their faith was, "What spiritual blessings are instore for Christians after conversion?" Pentecostals believe that God wants every believer to be filled with the power of the Holy Spirit, which is an experience that mainly occurs after conversion. Today, you will learn the meaning of Pentecost and the fundamental teachings of the Pentecostal movement.

1. What is Pentecost?

The word *Pentecost* means "the fiftieth day." Both Jews and Christians celebrate Pentecost. Among the Jewish people, Pentecost is a harvest festival celebrated fifty days after another festival called the Passover. The Passover is the celebration that marks the emancipation of Israel from Egypt (Exodus 12). However, in the Christian tradition, Pentecost happens fifty days after Easter, which is the season when Christians remember the death, burial, and resurrection of Jesus.

According to Acts 2:1-13, God poured out His Spirit on the disciples on the day of Pentecost, fifty days after Jesus was raised from the dead. The disciples were all together in one place, in the upper room in Jerusalem, when tongues of fire rested on each of them, and "they were filled with the Holy Ghost" (Acts 2:3-4). The moment they were filled with the living presence of the Holy Spirit they all spoke with other tongues (2:4). That event marks the birth of the church, and it continues to rest at the heart of the church and our faith.

2. What is Pentecostalism?

Pentecostalism is a movement within Christianity that believes in the direct personal experience of the living Holy Spirit. It seeks to restore the spiritual power and mission that existed in the early church, as seen in the book of Acts. As we know it today, Pentecostalism was influenced by a group of believers who left the Methodist church in the late 19th century in the USA and formed a movement called the Christian Union. Those believers wanted to live a life completely surrendered to God, so they went on a spiritual search for a deeper level of sanctification and holiness of life.

By 1906 under the leadership of a black preacher named William J. Seymour, God poured out the Holy Spirit on believers at Azusa Street, Los Angeles, USA. This was a wonderful time of spiritual revival, witnessing, and miracles for the glory of God. The 1906 revival marks the beginning of the spread of Pentecostalism around the world.

3. Key beliefs of Pentecostalism

Let us now look at three critical beliefs of Pentecostalism. Most Pentecostal churches accept the following beliefs as part of their understanding of the Christian faith:

a. Pentecostals believe in the direct personal experience of the Holy Spirit and fire. This experience is thought of as the baptism of the Spirit. Pentecostals accept that this is a work of grace after conversion (we will review some passages below). Pentecostals believe the baptism of the Holy Spirit is still available to believers today. Each believer must seek earnestly and pray passionately for the empowering of the Holy Spirit.

b. Pentecostals accept that being filled with the Holy Spirit is a personal experience that is followed by speaking in other tongues as the Spirit gives utterance. This experience occurs after conversion based on one's devotion to God and is an empowerment for service. Pentecostals largely believe that speaking in tongues is the initial or visible evidence of receiving the gift of the Spirit and power (Acts 2:38). Along with tongues, believers receive other spiritual gifts, such as faith, healing, and discernment from the Holy Spirit in preparation for service and witnessing for God.

c. Pentecostals believe that every born-again Christian should seek personal sanctification. Sanctification literally means "to make holy, set apart, or purify." It involves separation and deliverance from personal sin and consecration to God. This does not mean absolute sinless perfection, as seen in the life of Christ. Instead, it is a thorough inner cleansing of the heart and soul until the believer is fully yielded to God. Sanctification is done through a life of disciplined living and constant avoidance of wrongdoing. In Leviticus 11:44, God says, "For I am the Lord your God: ye shall therefore sanctify yourselves, and ye shall be holy; for I am holy."

The experience of the Holy Spirit flows from a life that is pure and fully surrendered to God. The baptism of the Holy Spirit is an inheritance in store for those who live in the light of the Lord, are forgiven, and sanctified by faith in Jesus (Acts 26:18).

4. **Important passages for Pentecostalism**

Several passages in the book of Acts speak directly about receiving the Holy Spirit. Luke, the writer of this book describes the same experience in different ways: being "*baptized* in the Holy Spirit" (1:5); "the Holy Spirit is *come upon you"* (1:8); being *"filled with the Holy Spirit"* (2:4); and you will "*receive the gift* of the Holy Spirit" (2:38)

All these passages refer to the same experience of receiving the Holy Spirit, which Jesus promised to His disciples (Acts 1:4-9). In Acts 2:1-4, 33, and 38, we have separate accounts of Jesus" disciples receiving the outpouring of the Spirit. One example is the coming of the Spirit on a man named Cornelius and his family in Acts 10:44-49.

Pentecostals believe that what happened in the early church on the day of Pentecost and at the turn of the 1900s is one continuous act of God pouring His Spirit on His people. We believe that the revivals of the 1900s fulfilled what the Apostle Peter said in Acts 2:29. "For the promise is unto you, and to your children, and to all that are afar off, even as many as the Lord our God shall call." (Acts 2:39).

Summary and Life Application

The direct experience of baptism in the Holy Spirit is the spiritual center of Pentecostal teaching and identity. Pentecostals believe Christians should seek holiness of life and the baptism of the Spirit. Would you like to receive the baptism of the Holy Spirit? You should seek after a personal experience and baptism in the Holy Spirit. All Christians should receive the infilling of the Holy Spirit after (or at the point of) converting their lives to Jesus. How do you know if you have been filled with the Holy Spirit? Pentecostals believe the evidence of speaking in tongues is the visible sign of Holy Spirit baptism. The Spirit is God's power for service and living in the world. Do not attempt to live the Christian life without the baptism of the Spirit.

LESSON 16—WEEKLY ASSIGNMENT

Spend some time to pray and seek after the gift of the Holy Spirit. Increase your passion and desire for a life of holiness as you ask God to cleanse all known sins from your life. Invite other believers to pray with you for this gift. Seek and ask in faith for the gift of the Spirit.

Pray this Prayer

Father, fill me with the Spirit and fire. I believe the gift of the Spirit is your promise to me. The Spirit was given to help me serve you and live for you in this world. Allow your Spirit to be poured out in my life as you did on the Day of Pentecost. I want my life to be filled with the power and anointing of the Holy Spirit. Grant the Holy Spirit as a gift to me. Amen.

LESSON 17

Declaration of Faith – Part 1

Introduction

Welcome to another lesson in this discipleship study series. The following four lessons will cover the Declaration of Faith, an official document of the Church of God. The Declaration of Faith consists of the core teachings, beliefs, and doctrines that the Church of God embraces as its statement of faith. A statement of faith is an official or public announcement or declaration of belief. Each lesson will cover three or four statements adapted in 1948 at the General Assembly of the Church of God. A statement of faith can be important on three levels:

1. It can help converts to know the particular beliefs they will embrace.
2. It is a way of telling other people what we believe as practicing Christians.
3. It can be used as an indicator to know whether an organization represents true Christianity.

The Declaration of Faith has fourteen articles or statements. Today, you cover the first four.

Article 1:_*We believe in the verbal inspiration of the Bible*

The "verbal inspiration" of the Bible means two things; first, *verbal* means every word of the Bible is a communication from God's breath. Second, *inspiration* refers to the fact that the Spirit of God guided the writers of the Bible to record God's will.

a. The verbal inspiration of the Bible. Paul says, "All Scripture is given by inspiration of God" (2 Timothy 3:16). Verbal inspiration means the Bible came from the breath of God. Thus, the words and ideas of the Bible are accurate and represent God's will. The Old Testament is a collection of inspired writings. The prophets often declared, "Thus says the Lord." God also inspired the writings in the New Testament. Paul confirmed that his teachings were not from man's wisdom but from the Holy Ghost (1 Corinthians 2:13).

b. The Holy Spirit inspired the Bible. The whole Bible owes its origin to the work of the Holy Spirit. The Bible did not come from the will of man, "but holy men of God spoke as they were moved by the Holy Spirit" (2 Peter 1:21). All the words, phrases, sentences work together to give us God's message and are purposefully there for our benefit.

The Bible is God's inspired word. You can trust the Bible as God's Holy Word. It does not mean God condones all the actions in the Bible. Everything in the Bible is there to teach you something about history and God's will. We need to depend on the Spirit to interpret the Bible.

Article 2: *We believe in one God eternally existing in three persons: namely, the Father, Son, and Holy Ghost.*

Article number two expresses a belief in the doctrine that God exists as three persons. This teaching is known to us as the Trinity.

a. God is One. Deuteronomy 6:4 declares, "Hear, O Israel: The LORD our God, is one LORD." The Bible teaches that there is a God, and God is one. It is best to understand this statement as announcing the complete uniqueness of God. This is a statement against idolatry. God is one, yet three. God's oneness means there is no other like Jehovah.

b. However, the Bible reveals God existing as three—a compound unity—meaning the Father, Son, and Spirit share the same divine nature. God as one-yet-three divine beings. The prophet Isaiah speaks as if it were the Messiah speaking of His sending forth by the Father and the Spirit, "there am I: and now the Lord God, and his Spirit, hath sent me" (48:16).

We see another example of God as a Holy Trinity in Matthew 3:16-17, where the Holy Spirit descended upon Jesus, and the Father spoke from heaven. Each member of the Trinity has a specific role: the Father—Creator and source of all things; the Son—redeems us from sin and death; the Holy Spirit—regenerates and empowers.

The doctrine of God as one-yet-three is the foundation of the Christian faith. We must boldly accept and affirm this profound mystery. The God of the Christian Bible is unique.

Article 3: *We believe that Jesus Christ is the only begotten Son of the Father, conceived of the Holy Ghost, and born of the Virgin Mary. That Jesus was crucified, buried, and raised from the dead. That He ascended to heaven and is today at the right hand of the Father as the Intercessor.*

This article summarizes the story of salvation through Jesus Christ.

We believe that Jesus is the only begotten Son of the Father. The heavenly Father is described as "the God and Father of our Lord Jesus Christ" (Ephesians 1:3). God the Father has begotten (or given life to) Jesus. We are not able to explain it fully in this life.

a. We accept the incarnation and virgin birth of Jesus. Jesus was conceived of the Holy Ghost and born of the Virgin Mary (Luke 1:30-35). The *incarnation* refers to the union of God and man. It literally means "in the flesh." Christ was supernaturally conceived. In Matthew, an angel of the Lord told Joseph, "for that which is conceived in her is of the Holy Spirit" (1:20). Through the incarnation, God–in the person of Jesus Christ–became flesh. Paul said, in Jesus, "God was manifest in the flesh" (1 Timothy 3:16).

b. Jesus was crucified. God "spared not his own Son but delivered Him up for us all" (Romans 8:32). Jesus was our substitute on the cross. He "gave Himself for our sins, that He might deliver us from this present evil world" (Galatians 1:4). Jesus was raised from the dead. The resurrection of Jesus is a true historical event. Christ appeared to His disciples after He had been raised from death (John 20:27).

c. Jesus ascended to heaven. Jesus did not remain on earth, but He ascended to heaven and is today at the right hand of God as the Intercessor. The apostle Paul describes the living Christ's position of power in Romans 8:34, "It is Christ that died, yea rather, that is risen again, who is even at the right hand of God, who also maketh intercession for us."

Jesus died for our salvation, and now He lives forever to make intercession for us. His constant concern and prayers offer us comfort in life's tribulations. He remains as our intercessor in heaven.

Article 4: *We believe that all have sinned and come short of the glory of God and that repentance is commanded of God for all and necessary for forgiveness of sins.*

It is the belief of the church that we have all sinned against God. According to 1 John 3:4, sin is breaking the laws of God. We sin in relation to other people through immoral conduct against and with one another. Concerning oneself, sin is self-centeredness or personal pride.

Sin is universal. Romans 3:23 says, "For all have sinned and fallen short of the glory of God." No one is innocent. We are all guilty of falling short of God's will; thus, repentance is necessary for forgiveness. The word for repentance means, "to change one's mind and attitude toward God and sin." To be saved from sin, there must be "repentance toward God and faith in our Lord Jesus Christ" (Acts 20:21).

Repentance and faith go hand in hand. In Christianity, faith and repentance must come before forgiveness. We must repent and have faith in Jesus before we receive God's forgiveness.

Summary and Life Application

As a Christian, you must know that the whole Bible is the Word of God. The Holy Spirit inspired the Bible. As you read your Bible, trust the Spirit to guide you into the truth of God's word. The Bible reveals to us that God is one, yet three; God is the Holy Trinity. God wants your total devotion to Him alone. There is no God like Jehovah. Jesus is the clearest manifestation of God in the flesh. He died in your place so that you can find forgiveness for all your sins. If you sin, what must you do to be forgiven? Do not live your Christian life with unconfessed sins.

LESSON 17—WEEKLY ASSIGNMENT

Use the week to write out and memorize the four Statements of Faith.

LESSON 18

Declaration of Faith: Articles 5 – 8

Introduction

This is another exciting week. The aim is to continue to grow deeper in the Christian faith. Do you remember the articles you learned about in the last lesson? It is helpful to keep in mind that these articles are statements of faith. Their purpose is to help build your convictions about some of the most critical themes in the Bible. Of course, over time, you will develop more than fourteen core beliefs. Christianity is built on beliefs (or teachings), and these beliefs can give us a clear vision of what we stand for and where we are going. Today, you will learn articles 5 – 8 and understand the provisions of God for our salvation.

Article 5: *We believe that justification, regeneration, and the new birth are wrought by faith in the blood of Jesus Christ.*

This article points to the initial experience of salvation. One must understand that true salvation includes justification and regeneration by faith in Jesus. These provisions are given to you at the moment of conversion.

a. What is the meaning of *justification*? Justification means that God freely gives a sinner who believes in Christ a right standing before Him. Justification comes about in two ways. First, a man is justified by faith, not by his works (Romans 3:28). God declares us righteous because of our faith in Jesus Christ. Faith is a personal act on our part. Second, we are justified by grace: "Being justified freely by His grace through the redemption that is in Christ" (Romans 3:24).

   The grace of God makes it possible for us to stand before God. Through justification, we have peace with God. "Therefore, being justified by faith, we have peace with God through our Lord Jesus Christ" (Romans 5:1). This means our relationship with God has been restored. We are no longer enemies of God but now His children.

a. To a Christian, what does *regeneration* mean? Regeneration refers to "being born again or the new birth." Through regeneration, God changes your old nature and creates a new spiritual life within you. Regeneration is entirely the act of God; we cannot observe when it happens because it is The Holy Spirit who regenerates us. Jesus taught, "You must be born again" (John 3:7). In the new birth, the Holy Spirit washes away our sins and renews us spiritually.

b. Once regenerated, the believer receives a new "divine nature" (2 Peter 1:4). That does not mean you become gods or immortal. It simply means God's spirit transforms our moral character. Now, the Spirit of God lives in us, giving us the power to overcome evil desires. In regeneration, God acts as a surgeon, while in justification, He serves as a judge. Regeneration signals the beginning of a new life, and justification helps us overcome our guilt before God.

Where we deserved condemnation, God's grace says, "You are right with me." Justification changes our relationship with God into one of peaceful standing. How does that make you feel?

Article 6: *We believe in sanctification subsequent to the new birth, through faith in the blood of Christ; through the Word, and by the Holy Ghost.*

Article 7: *We believe holiness to be God's standard of living for His people.*

Articles six (6) and seven (7) are similar; therefore, we will cover them together. What provisions of God should follow Christians after their conversion? We believe in a life of sanctification and holiness.

a. What is *sanctification*? The word sanctification means holiness or separation from unclean things. Sanctification begins at salvation, where God breaks the power of sin over our lives. However, sanctification continues throughout our Christian journey. Do you know how believers are sanctified? Sanctification comes through Jesus Christ. Hebrews 10:10 says we are "sanctified through the blood of Jesus Christ once for all." The blood of Jesus cleanses us from all sin.

b. Sanctification comes through the Word. Christ prayed to the Father, "Sanctify them through your truth. Thy word is truth" (John 17:17). Sanctification comes through the Holy Spirit. 2 Thessalonians 2:13 says that God has "chosen you to salvation through sanctification of the Spirit and belief of the truth." The Spirit works in our lives to bring about holiness of heart unto God.

c. Sanctification comes through our actions. The people of God are to stay away from everything sinful. Joshua commanded Israel, saying, "sanctify yourselves, for tomorrow the Lord will do wonders among you" (Joshua 3:5).

Every aspect of our being—soul, spirit, and body—is to be submitted to God in complete holiness. The Bible expects us to practice sanctification or holiness practically. We are to abstain from all wrongdoings and live pure for the glory of God.

Article 8: *We believe in the baptism with the Holy Ghost subsequent to a clean heart.*

This is our final article for today. As Christians, we believe in the baptism of the Holy Spirit. Let us explore some important works of the Holy Spirit in our life:

a. The Holy Spirit indwells believers. Each believer receives the Holy Spirit at conversion. The Holy Spirit helps to nurture our Christian life and bestows new spiritual abilities within us. The Spirit of God allows us to develop the "fruit of the Spirit." The fruit of the Spirit is: love, joy, peace, longsuffering, gentleness, goodness, faith, meekness, and temperance (Galatians 5:22- 23). These fruits help us to mature into the character of Christ.

b. The Spirit gives us other special gifts. These are spiritual abilities such as power, wisdom, healing, discernment, tongues, and so forth (1 Corinthians 12:4-11, Romans 12:6-8). Spiritual gifts are God-given abilities to serve the church, while the fruit of the Spirit is character qualities that shape us into the image of Christ. You need both to be at work in you.

c. The Holy Spirit empowers believers through baptism with the Holy Ghost. This intense spiritual experience is available to all believers (Acts 2:1-4). As a Christian, you should expect and seek the baptism of the Holy Spirit. Spirit baptism is called "the promise of the Father." God promised by the prophet Joel (2:28-29) that He would pour out His Spirit on all flesh in the last days.

d. Spirit baptism is spoken of as being "filled with the Holy Spirit" (Acts 2:4). On the day of Pentecost, when God poured out his Spirit on the disciples, their spirits were entirely under the control of the Spirit of God. Being filled with the Spirit is an overflowing experience. Spirit baptism is described as an "outpouring," emphasizing the abundance with which God bestows the Holy Spirit unto believers (Acts 2:17-18).

e. The baptism of the Spirit occurs after conversion. God may give this special blessing immediately following our conversion or sometime after our conversion experience. When we are converted, Jesus brings us into a relationship with God through the baptism of the Spirit, making us a part of the family of God. Every believer receives the Spirit the moment they trust in Jesus for salvation (John 7:38-39).

Being filled with the Spirit is a repeatable experience. It is available for all believers. The filling of the Spirit is the controlling influence of God within the believer. As Pentecostals, we believe that every member should seek after the baptism or infilling of the Spirit with tongues of fire and power. In the church, some congregations encourage new believers to tarry for the Spirit. That means spending time in fasting and prayer until you are filled with the Spirit of God.

Summary and Life Application

The gift of salvation is God's wonderful provision for all those who trust in Jesus as Savior. As part of the experience of salvation, God justifies and regenerates all believers. Justification is God declaring us guilt-free. As our heavenly judge, God says you are free in Christ. He regenerates us - you have a new moral and spiritual life in Jesus. These two blessings work together and occur at the beginning of our salvation. That is not all. After our conversion, God expects us to live holy and entirely sold-out for Him. Your sanctification is an ongoing process. Each day, you should live for God and separate yourself from all evil.

Further, God wants to fill you with the power of the Spirit. You must actively seek the gift of the Spirit, through fasting and prayer and a life entirely devoted to God. Would you like to be filled with the Holy Spirit?

LESSON 18—WEEKLY ASSIGNMENT

Read the following passages before the next class: Philippians 1:9-11; 1 Corinthians 12:4-11, 18-21; Romans 12:6-9.

Use the week to write out and memorize articles 5–8.

In your own words, what do you think happens to believers when they are filled with the Spirit?

____

____

____

____

LESSON 19

Declaration of Faith: Articles 9 – 11

Introduction

What makes these lessons on the articles of faith important is their celebration of doctrine-in-practice. That means that doctrines (the church's primary teachings) are only helpful if they guide us into a personal relationship with Jesus. Today, we will be looking at three additional teachings that the Church of God holds and practices. You will learn about a Christian experience called speaking in tongues. You will also study water baptism and the atonement. We will begin by exploring the Bible's teachings on speaking with other tongues.

Article 9: *We believe in speaking with other tongues as the Spirit gives utterance and that it is the initial evidence of the baptism of the Holy Ghost.*

What does it mean to speak in tongues? Speaking in (or with) tongues involves an individual being given the ability to speak in an unknown spiritual language. That language may or may not be understood by someone else. It is the Spirit of God that makes it possible to speak in tongues.

a. Is speaking in tongues the initial evidence of the baptism in the Holy Spirit? On several occasions in the book of Acts, when the Spirit came, believers spoke in tongues. When the Holy Spirit came, the first recognizable sign among the disciples was that they spoke in tongues (Acts 2:1-4). The crowd heard Peter and the other disciples speak in several known languages, even though those languages were previously unknown.

The Caesarean Gentile believers also received the gift of the Holy Spirit. Peter and other Jews heard "them speak with tongues and magnify God" (Acts 10:46). From all indications, speaking in spiritual tongues is the first recognizable evidence of Spirit baptism.

b. Why is speaking in tongues so important? In addition to being the initial evidence of Spirit baptism, tongues are otherwise important. It is a form of communication with God in prayer and praise. God can use spiritual tongues as a message or sign to those who do not believe in Christ (1 Corinthians 14:22). It shows to unbelievers that God is doing a work among believers. Speaking in tongues is also a sign that we live in the time called the "Last Days" (Acts 2:17; 3:18-26). God made a promise to give this gift to believers in the last days.

c. Is Spirit baptism only for mature believers? No. Spirit baptism is a gift from God to all believers. All believers should have a desire for this wonderful experience. Soon after becoming a Christian or along the way of the Christian walk, one may receive the baptism of the Spirit. God gives this gift to any believer who actively seeks after this gift. Repentance and water baptism are the basic requirements for receiving the baptism in the Holy Spirit (Acts 2:38).

Those whose hearts have been prepared by the Holy Spirit will receive the experience of Spirit baptism. The Baptism of the Spirit is a gift for all believers and not a privilege reserved for a few persons. Do you believe you are ready at this point to receive the gift of the Spirit?

Article 10: *We believe in water baptism by immersion, and all who repent should be baptized in the name of the Father, and of the Son, and of the Holy Ghost.*

Water baptism is more than a religious ceremony—it is a pledge to God and to others that we will devote ourselves to Christ-like living. Water baptism portrays the union of the believer with Christ in His death and resurrection.

a. Water baptism symbolizes forgiveness and cleansing from sin, and our new life that we received through faith in Christ (Mark 1:5). Jesus commanded his disciples to carry out water baptisms. Christ authorized His disciples to baptize all those who believe His teachings. "Go therefore and make disciples of all the nations, baptizing them in the name of the Father and of the Son and of the Holy Spirit" (Matt. 28:19).

b. Baptism in water is to be done "in the name of the Father and of the Son and of the Holy Spirit." Why should baptisms be done in the name of each member of the Holy Trinity? This is because all three share in the life and salvation of humans. The Father is the ultimate Creator and Ruler of all earthly life and affairs. The Son is the Redeemer and forgiver of sins; we are saved because of His death. The Spirit gives us the new birth and brings us into the Father's family.

Water baptism is a public testimony of our conversion and obedience to Christ's command. All who believe in Jesus should be baptized. We accept that the Father, Son, and Spirit work together to bring about our salvation. How do you think baptism can inspire you as a Christian?

Article 11: *We believe divine healing is provided for all in the atonement.*

Among the benefits of the cross of Jesus are physical, emotional, mental, and spiritual healing. The atonement speaks to Christ's sacrifice for our sins to restore us to the right relationship with God.

a. The gospel is not a guarantee that we will escape all earthly suffering. In fact, suffering is a grace by which we are made more perfect in our relationship with Jesus. "For unto you it is given in the behalf of Christ, not only to believe on him, but also to suffer for his sake" (Philippians 1:29).

b. As part of the remedy for sin, God makes provisions for us to receive divine healing. Divine healing comes through the total ministry of Christ and has been provided for everyone through his death. The fact that the risen Jesus provides healing is one of the great truths of Scripture.

c. Healing is an expression of Christ's sympathy for suffering people. On many occasions, we are told, Jesus was "moved with compassion" as He healed their diseases (Matthew 9:36). Jesus Christ has the power to forgive sins, to rescue from eternal death, and to heal our diseases. Healing is a sign that when God resurrects believers from the dead at the return of Christ, they will be completely healed (1 Corinthians 15:35-55).

   Sometimes in our sickness, God works miracles in our lives by bringing good out of our suffering. God can use sickness to deepen our faith and trust in Him. God's provision of healing does not mean that everyone will be healed all the time and from every illness. Scripture does not support that claim.

d. Although God never creates evil, He often uses our struggles to accomplish His purpose. In 2 Corinthians 12: 9-10, God said the Paul, "My grace is sufficient for thee: for my strength is made perfect in weakness." What was Paul's response? "I rather glory in my infirmities, that the power of Christ may rest upon me...**10**for when I am weak, then am I strong.

What should believers do when confronted with illness? We should pray! We are to trust and hope in God. At times, answers to our prayers may take weeks, months, or even years and require us to be patient and persistent. However, God gives us the strength to pray in our suffering.

Summary and Life Application

As we bring this lesson to a close, remember that God has made many provisions for you as a Christian. He desires to fill you with the power of this Holy Spirit. Spiritual tongues are a sign, and according to the experiences in Acts, it is the initial evidence that you are filled with the Spirit. Do not live your life without seriously seeking God for this experience. Partner with a fellow believer to seek the baptism of the Holy Spirit. This experience is for you as much as it is for mature believers. In addition, you identify with Christ through your baptism; take your baptism seriously. Finally, as a child of God, when you feel sick, pray to God for divine healing. Call upon the elders, your pastor, or other believers to seek God for deliverance. Jesus is compassionate to the sick. However, if God does not provide immediate healing, remember that the grace that sustains us through suffering is greater than if God simply erased all difficulties from our life.

LESSON 19—WEEKLY ASSIGNMENT

Spend some time praying for the baptism of the Holy Spirit. Trust the Spirit to fill you and give you the ability to speak with spiritual tongues. Pray to God for healing if you are sick and believe that God can heal you.

Continue to memorize the Articles of Faith.

LESSON 20

Declaration of Faith: Articles 12 – 14

Introduction

Welcome to the final official lesson of this series. Today, you will be covering the last of the articles of faith. Remember, the more you know, the more you will understand the Bible and deepen your walk with the Lord. These things will become more apparent to you in time, but you must start your walk as a Christian with the proper preparation. In this lesson, you will learn about the Lord's Supper and the washing of the saints' feet. You will also understand certain events that will lead up toward the return of Jesus and what follows.

Article 12: *We believe in the Lord's Supper and Washing of the Saints" Feet.*

Just before His death, Jesus instituted the Lord's Supper and the washing of His disciples" Feet. The Lord's Supper is also known as "Holy Communion." Both practices are also known as ordinances or sacraments, for they carry special spiritual values for Christians.

a. The Lord's Supper is a meal that Christians share to remember Christ's death, resurrection, and glorious return in the future. It is also a sign of God's continued favor and love toward the New Covenant and us. Jesus instituted the Lord's Supper. When Jesus sat with his disciples for their last meal together, He took bread, broke and blessed it, gave it to His disciples, and said: "This is my body which is given for you: this do in remembrance of me" (Luke 22:19).

   Then He took the cup, saying, "This cup is the New Testament in my blood, which is shed for you" (Luke 22: 20). The Lord's Supper honors Jesus; "this do ye, as oft as ye drink it, in remembrance of me" (1 Corinthians 11:25). It is a sign of our fellowship with Christ and each other. Jesus instituted the Lord's Supper for all believers, including the newly repentant and seasoned Christians.

b. Jesus washed His disciples" feet and instructed them to continue the practice. By washing His disciples" feet, Jesus portrayed a spirit of service (John 13:1-17). Foot-washing points to our fellowship with Jesus Christ. Jesus told Peter, "If I do not wash you, you have no part with Me" (John 13:8). Foot-washing calls us to humility and service.

As followers of Jesus, we are to follow His example. All believers are eligible to participate in the Lord's Supper and foot-washing. You do not need to be perfect to share in these sacred activities.

Article 13: *We believe in the premillennial second coming of Jesus. First, to resurrect the righteous dead and to catch away the living saints to Him in the air. Second, to reign on the earth one thousand years.*

Article 14: *We believe in the bodily resurrection; eternal life for the righteous, and eternal punishment for the wicked.*

These final two articles point us to some events that will happen at the end of this age. As believers, we rest on the New Testament hope of the Second Coming of Christ. The meaning of a *premillennial* coming of Jesus has to do with teaching that He will physically return to earth before the millennium—one thousand years of peace on earth.

a. We believe that Jesus is coming again. In John 14:3, Jesus promises His disciples, "And if I go and prepare a place for you, I will come again, and receive you unto myself; that where I am, there ye may also be." Also, in Acts 1:10, as Jesus" followers watched Him ascend toward heaven, an angel appeared and reassured them, "why stand ye gazing up into heaven? this same Jesus, which is taken up from you into heaven, shall so come in like manner as ye have seen him go into heaven" (Acts 1:11)

The early believers looked forward to the return of Jesus. We live a life that is sober and godly, "Looking for that blessed hope, and the glorious appearing of the great God and our Savior Jesus Christ" (Titus 2:13). The book of Revelation ends with a personal address from Jesus to the church, "Sure, I come quickly" (22:20). His final words are that His return is very close.

b. When is Jesus coming? The Bible tells us "But of that day and hour knoweth no man" (Matthew 24:36). However, we have some details to help us understand the events that will happen. For instance, we know what Jesus" return will be in two phases.

Phase 1: Jesus will return in the air to resurrect and caught up the saints.

1 Thessalonians 4:16-17, "For the Lord himself shall descend from heaven with a shout, with the voice of the archangel, and with the trump of God: and the dead in Christ shall rise first: [17] Then we which are alive and remain shall be caught up together with them in the clouds, to meet the Lord in the air: and so shall we ever be with the Lord."

At the resurrection, Jesus will transform the bodies of believers who have died and those still living on earth, changing their earthly bodies to heavenly bodies (1 Corinthians 15:51-52). At the resurrection, our bodies will change from mortal to immortal. In other words, we will have eternal life.

This event will not be a secret. At Christ's return, all eyes will see Him. Revelation states, "Behold, he cometh with clouds; and every eye shall see him, and they also which pierced him: and all kindreds of the earth shall wail because of him" (Revelation 1:7).

Phase 2: Jesus will physically return to earth before His Millennial Reign. Before Christ returns however, a series of events are to take place leading up to His return. There will be a time of great troubles on the earth (often referred to as the great tribulation), which will be followed by the battle of Armageddon.

What is the great tribulation? The great tribulation is a time of intense suffering that is coming on the earth. The prophet Daniel predicted this in Daniel 9 as a period that will last for seven years. Jesus told His disciples to expect it; "For then shall be great tribulation, such as was not since the beginning of the world to this time, no, nor ever shall be" (Matthew 24:21). During the Tribulation, an evil person opposed to Christ will appear and deceive many. The Bible refers to this evil man as the "son of perdition," "the lawless one," and "the Antichrist" (2 Thessalonians 2:3-8; 1 John 4:2-3). Through his lies, the anti-Christ will lead many to reject Christ. Revelation 7:14 says that some people will be saved after "the great tribulation."

What happens after the great tribulation? The Bible says the Battle of Armageddon. Before Christ sets up His Kingdom, a great army will seek to wage war against Him. This war will be known as the Battle of Armageddon. It will bring about the doom of both the world ruler (known in Revelation as the "beast") and His "false prophet." These two will be "cast alive into the lake of fire burning with brimstone" (Revelation 19:20).

The Second coming and the millennial reign of Christ. The Tribulation will reach its conclusion when Jesus Christ comes to earth to reign for a thousand years. We believe that Christ's Second Coming will occur before His Millennial Reign, a view called "premillennialism." Christ's return will precede His thousand-year reign on the earth. Both the Old and New Testaments speak of a time when Christ will reign on the Earth for a thousand years (Revelation 20:4- 6).

The release and defeat of Satan will happen at the end of the one-thousand-year reign of Christ. At the bidding of God, Satan will be released from his prison and will go out to deceive the nations which are in the four corners of the earth (Revelation 20:7-8). He will seek to lead a major rebellion, but Christ will defeat Him forever. The Final Judgment of all unbelievers will also occur after the Millennium, following the resurrection of unbelievers (2 Peter 2:9).

In the Final Judgment, those who believe in Christ will not experience condemnation, but the wicked and unbelieving will be condemned from the presence of God.

Summary and Life Application

As a Christian, each time you share in the Lord's Supper you are remembering the sacrifice of Christ. Never forget what Jesus has done for you. Do not brush-off invitations to share in this sacred meal. Doing so is an insult to the Lord. In addition, remember that the Christian life is to be a life of humble service to each other, as we all wait in hope of the return of Christ.

LESSON 20—WEEKLY ASSIGNMENT

Continue to memorize the articles of faith.

LESSON 21

Next Steps

Introduction

Congratulations, you have done it. You have completed this discipleship series. This is an important milestone for you. How are you feeling? As we approach the end of this discipleship program, I want you to know that the local church is here to support you. The purpose of this session is to help you understand your next steps. The plan at this point is to get you united with the membership of your church. If you have not yet done so, your next step should be your reception in the fellowship of believers in the local congregation where you worship. As we plan for that, we will also complete a simple spiritual group test. This is not an exam or a competition. There are no right or wrong answers, only true answers. It is a test to help you think about your Christian growth and areas of possible development.

Church Membership

As a Christian, church membership is vital to your continued growth. The church typically welcomes new members during a special service. There you will receive what is commonly called the *right hand of fellowship,* which is a sign that you are now an official member of the local church. Why is church membership important? Being a member of a local church gift you with a place where you can be spiritually led, biblically fed, and lovingly protected by gifted leaders. The Bible requires more than just casual or under-the-radar membership; it calls us into a covenant community (Acts 2: 41-47).

Joining ministry Groups

There are several small groups or ministry groups in your church. You might be familiar with these groups already. They include ladies, men, youth, teens, children, couples, choirs, Sunday School, Bible Studies, fasting, among others. Your discipleship mentor will help you to get to know these ministry groups. These ministry groups are there for you. The discipleship team will help assign you to one or more of the groups.

Do not delay joining the ministry groups at your church. It is recommended that you make it a habit to attend the scheduled meetings for these groups. Commit yourself to habitually attend Bible Studies for the next six months and beyond. Joining a ministry group is not an option, it is a necessity.

Spiritual Growth Assessment

This test helps you to think carefully about your spiritual growth. Before completing your responses, ask the Lord to guide your evaluation.

Spiritual Growth Assessment	
As you complete the assessment, avoid rushing. Use the scale below to respond to each statement. **No– 1 Probably not – 2 Sometimes – 3 Usually – 4 Yes– 5**	
Spiritual Disciplines	**Response**
Conversion	
1. I believe Jesus is the Son of God and that He is the only way to salvation	
2. I am committed to living as a Christian and being consistent in my walk with God	
3. I remain confident in my salvation and growing in my relationship with God	
Conversion Total	
Disciplines	
1. I regularly read and study my Bible as the guide for the way I think and act	
2. I regularly spend time in personal prayer listening to and praising God	

3. If I sin, I quickly repent, trust God for forgiveness, and strive to live holy	
Disciplines Total	
Character	
1. I am growing in love, patience, joy, gentleness, and in Christian courage	
2. I am moderate in my behavior, seek to be a spiritual example and loyal to family	
3. I depend on the Holy Spirit to help me resist temptation	
Character Total	
Purpose	
1. I know my purpose is to worship, witness, and work for God's glory	
2. I share my faith in Christ with non-believers	
3. I am trusting God to fill me with the Holy Spirit and to use my life for His glory	
Purpose Total	
Community	
1. I commit to regularly attend church and embrace the teachings of the church	
2. I love my church and I am committed to protecting its purity and witness	
3. I sacrificially contribute my finances to my church and for the glory of God	
Community Total	
Faith and Hope	
1. I am prepared to share my testimony with non-Christians	
2. I have made up my mind and have no intentions of turning my back on God	
3. I am determined to "finish the race", being faithful to Jesus until He returns.	
Faith and Hope Total	

Compare your results with another member. How do you feel about your progress as a Christian? Is there any area of growth or improvement for you? How can you continue to grow?

Continue to Grow

1. Attend a worship service weekly.
2. Memorize a scripture verse each week and take notes from sermons and Bible studies.
3. Spend time in prayer and praise to God.
4. Build healthy relationship with believers and non-believers.
5. Seek to discover your spiritual gifts and use them for the glory of God.
6. Work with a spiritual mentor who can help you grow in your faith.
7. Seek and embrace the Pentecostal experience of Spirit baptism.
8. Invite your family and friends to church so they can encounter Jesus as Savior.

Where do you see yourself serving in the church? For the next year, your duty is to deepen your growth in the Lord and your participation in the church.

Summary and Life Application

Once again, congratulations on completing this discipleship series. You have done well. You have spent the last twenty-one weeks growing and deepening your relationship with God. You have covered a lot of lessons and themes from the Bible. You have learned many disciplines and secrets of spiritual growth. We explored practical commitments and statements of faith we took from the Word of God. This entire program was designed to help you grow in the grace and knowledge of the Lord Jesus. Now that you are at the end remember, it does not stop here.

You are now ready to live the rest of your life for the glory of God. However, you can learn a lot more and so much more room to grow as a Christian. Live a life of holiness, power, and honesty before the Lord. In the words of the well-known Christian author Richard Foster, "In the spiritual life, only one thing produces genuine joy, and that is obedience." The journey continues! There is something more marvelous to come. Stay on the path, stick with the process, and remember this Christian journey is the greatest adventure that can ever undertake.

Supplement

A Short History of the Church of God International

The Church of God began on August 19, 1886, in Monroe County, Tennessee, near the North Carolina border. A former Baptist member, Richard Green Spurling, and eight devoted believers in a small millhouse along Barney Creek gathered together and formed what was known as the Christian Union. The purpose of the Christian Union was to follow the New Testament as a rule for faith and Christian practice. Twenty-one years later, the growing movement formally adopted the name the "*Church of God*" as its official designation.

Under the leadership of the first General Overseer, A. J. Tomlinson, the *Church of God* adopted a centralized form of church government with an inclusive International General Assembly (1906). By 1909, the *Church of God* launched a world evangelization effort beginning in The Bahamas.

Today, the *Church of God* reports more than 7 million members in 178 nations and territories, with some 36,000 congregations around the world. The Mission of the *Church of God* is to communicate the full gospel of Jesus Christ in the Spirit and power of Pentecost.

The New Testament Church of God, Jamaica

A preacher by the name, Rev. J. Wilson Bell from Kingston, Jamaica, was the first to contact the Church of God Headquarters in Cleveland, Tennessee, in the summer of 1917. The letter was an invitation for missionaries to be sent to Jamaica. In response, Tennessee sent Rev. J. S. Llewellyn in April 1918 to Jamaica. He, along with two Jamaican pastors—J. Wilson Bell and J. M. Parkinson—organized a church in Kingston with seven members.

In the following years, their service ultimately led to the planting of five (5) preaching stations, extending to Spanish Town, St Catherine, and by 1922 to the parish of Clarendon. On April 23, 1925, Bishop E. E. Simmonds came from Florida and was contacted by a local, H.A. Hudson. The latter directed him to a group worshipping in the community of Borobridge in the parish of Clarendon.

A partnership was established, which ultimately led to the official establishment and registration of the first local church with 62 members. During his 5-month trip, Bishop Simmonds established three churches, the other two being at Mount Providence and Frankfield (37 and 18 members respectively).

To register the church in Jamaica and the Caribbean, the *Church of God* had to modify its name to the *"New Testament Church of God"* because another denomination was already operating in the region with the name Church of God. By 1928, churches had been organized in several parishes. The first Island Convention was held from July 4-6, 1928, at Leicester Field in Clarendon. Seven churches and their Pastors attended.

Today, the New Testament Church of God has over 370 local congregations and it is the largest Pentecostal denomination on the island of Jamaica.

References

Arrington, French L. *Exploring the Declaration of Faith.* Cleveland, Tennessee: Pathway Press, 2003.

Church of God. Practical Commitments. Accessed February 12, 2016. Available from http://www.churchofgod.org/practical-commitments.

George, Bill. *Getting Started: New Beginnings in the Christian Life.* Cleveland, Tennessee: Pathway Press, 2001.

Into Thy Word. Discipleship Tools. Accessed January 16, 2016. Available from http://www.discipleshiptools.org/pages.asp?pageid=64826.

Riggs, Charles and Tom Phillips. *Thirty Discipleship Exercises: The Pathway to Christian Maturity*. Minneapolis, MN: 1980.

Warren, Rick. *The Purpose Driven Life: What on Earth am I Here For*? Grand Rapids, Michigan: Zondervan, 2002.

Made in the USA
Columbia, SC
15 December 2023

28664824R00072